LIGHTEN UP

LIGHTEN

U P

Survival Skills

for People Under

Pressure

C.W. Metcalf and
Roma Felible

A William Patrick Book

ADDISON-WESLEY PUBLISHING COMPANY
Reading, Massachusetts   Menlo Park, California   New York
Don Mills, Ontario   Wokingham, England   Amsterdam   Bonn
Sydney   Singapore   Tokyo   Madrid   San Juan
Paris   Seoul   Milan   Mexico City   Taipei

Library of Congress Cataloging-in-Publication Data

Metcalf, C. W. (Charles Willard)
    Lighten up : survival skills for people under pressure / C.W.
Metcalf and Roma Felible.
       p.   cm.
    Includes index.
    ISBN 0-201-56779-2
    ISBN 0-201-62239-4 (pbk.)
    1. Laughter. 2. Wit and humor—Psychological aspects. 3. Stress
management. I. Felible, Roma. II. Title.
BF575.L3M48 1992
152.4—dc20   91-41023
                                                  CIP

Cover photographs by Simon Metz
Interior photographs by Kevin Haislip

Cover design by Diana Coe
Text design by Joyce C. Weston
Set in 11-point Clarendon by Shepard Poorman Communications Corp.

1 2 3 4 5 6 7 8 9-MU-96959493
First printing, March 1992
First paperback printing, February 1993

Addison-Wesley books are available at special discounts for bulk purchases by corporations, institutions, and other organizations. For more information, please contact:

Special Markets Department
Addison-Wesley Publishing Company
Reading, MA 01867
(617) 944-3700 ext. 2431

For our parents, Roma B. and John E. Felible and Dorothy and Charles C. Metcalf, who taught us the strength of laughter, love, and forgiveness.

And for our silent partner, Harvey Brenner.

Contents

Acknowledgments, or Sharing the Blame

So that we will not be held solely responsible for this book's being written and published, we offer our thanks to the legions who encouraged or supported us or insisted that *Lighten Up* become a reality.

Without Harvey Brenner, Roma and I could never have written this work. It was Harvey who told me, "After all those years as a mime, C.W., you must have a lot of unused words hanging around—why not write 'em down and see if they add up to anything."

Without Jerry Jampolsky and the children and their families from the Center for Attitudinal Healing, I would have been left on the sidelines, never knowing how humor could heal. One family in particular, the Harrisons, were completely open in sharing their grief, strength, hope, and wisdom with me. Their son's life, not his death, still breathes in the book.

When Roma's parents, Roma B. and John, came to visit us in spring 1991, we asked if they would help with the manuscript. They agreed, and stayed until June. During that time they not only did their best to keep our syntax seamless and our spelling flawless, but also took care of us and our menagerie. If they hadn't, we might have starved to death before this project was done.

Of course, every Irish writer has to thank his mother. Dorothy Metcalf, through all my meandering, stumbling, stuttering "careers," never lost faith in me. When some thought I was nuts, she told me I was creative; when others thought I was incapable of making choices, she called me multitalented. Very early, when other mothers were hog-tying their children, she cut the strings that bound me to our matriarchal family.

"I never wanted anything for you, Butchie," she said, "except that you find something to do that makes you happy—and brings in enough money to buy me a motor home." Well, Mom, one out of two isn't so bad. And if enough of your friends buy this book, maybe you'll get the motor home, too.

Christian Hageseth III, M.D., was my original partner, and together we forged the prototype *Humor Option* seminars. He got foolish, I straightened up, and we did pretty well together. He was certainly the best and—okay—the only psychiatrist-mime I've ever known. From him, I learned more about acceptance and forgiveness than I thought possible. Without those lessons, my subsequent efforts would surely have failed.

Max Roby, professional fly fisherman, and Bill Benham—both of U.S. West Corporate Television—risked their fragile reputations, if not their jobs, to translate our early work into videotape form and thereby help thousands of people to lighten up.

Our office staff at C.W. Metcalf & Company contributed untold hours of phone calls, research, rewrites, and midnight mailings. Gaye Johnson, our office manager and vice-despot, never once said, "This is not in my job description." But, then, she doesn't have a job description. Our marketing madman, Steve Baumgartner, never complained that the erratic errands we sent him on (seeking some obscure reference to humor among the Patagonians) were beneath him. Truth be known, not that much is beneath Steve, anyway. Cynthia Geissinger, Mark Pearson, Nicky Marone, and Cynthia Marx contributed their talents in so many ways that it would be impossible to count them all.

The clients who risked so much to implement this approach in the corporate and health-care fields are the marrow of our success. To single out special clients is unfair, but I'll be unfair. Many clients helped us break new ground and find broader applications for Humor Skills. They are: Colorado State University; Hewlett-Packard; Herman Miller; AT&T; US West Corporate Television; International Business Machines; Mayo Affiliate Hospitals; South Hills Family Hospice of Pittsburgh (thanks, Lynn, for everything); Fort Collins (particularly, thanks to John Arnold and Barry Selberg) and Loveland, Colorado; Police Training Academy, Boulder, Colorado; Owens-Corning Fiberglas; Saturn Motor Company; American Hospital Association; Young President's Organization; National Broadcasters Association; British Columbia Department of Parks and Recreation; Blue Cross of California; Regent Hotel, Sydney, Australia; Strategic Air Command; and, far from last or least, Boondocks Medical Society.

Next to those first clients who had the foresight to hire us, the "financiers" who allowed us to grow took the biggest risk of all. Barry Lessinger loaned me an old suit—I had no suits at the time—and enough money to get business cards and stationery made. Bill and Evie Weddel invested in our business a few years later, allowing us to move out of the basement with its occasional flooding and into a real office. And, when not one financial institution on the planet would give us a nod, Phil Hitz at Security Pacific granted me a line of credit that allowed us to go international. (Yes, they've all been paid back. Okay, I kept the suit. Bell bottoms are bound to come back into style.)

When I began speaking as an unknown, agents naturally didn't return my phone calls. Now that the company is internationally recognized, agents call frequently. In the beginning, though, we had only Rickie Hall, of Rickie Hall & Associates in Boulder, Colorado, and she is still one of my two agents. She believed in me before I did, and led me to the other person who was willing to help build our company, Cheryl Miller of Speakers International in Chicago. These two women are the reasons I have clients and an audience for this book.

In a category by himself is Steve Berger. As President of Nationwide Communications, Inc., Steve supported our efforts in corporate and television endeavors. Most important, he taught me that business and friendship are not mutually exclusive.

Father Lawrence Martin Jenco helped us breathe life into the words of the Middle East hostages cited in *Lighten Up,* and led us to others who could help us understand the strengths that kept them sane. Psychologists Ken and Karen Druck also offered valuable input on the original manuscript.

William Patrick, our editor at Addison-Wesley, is a man of uncommon wit, intelligence, and insight. Roma and I are truly honored to be associated with one who brings intensity, personal attention, and vision to book editing.

I rarely agreed with our literary agent, Jane Dystal. I made her suggested changes in our book proposal only to prove her wrong. The book found a publisher. She was right; I was wrong. She's a genius; I'm a putz. Without her careful guidance and direction, *Lighten Up* would simply not exist.

(And, thank you, Bob Schmitz, for introducing us to Jane.)

Our thanks, too, to our attorneys, Tom Lamm and Patrick Butler of Lamm & Young. They didn't do much, but attorneys get so much bad press that we want to say something nice about these guys.

Finally, thank heaven, Roma and I want to thank each other. For life partners to build a successful business—especially when she's the President and CFO—is difficult enough. But to team up on writing a book, when she's the real writer, is a challenge no marriage should have to meet. Somehow we've come through it to rediscover a new dimension of loving and laughing together.

If you wish to glimpse inside a human soul and get to know a man . . . just watch him laugh. If he laughs well, he's a good man . . . .
    —*Dostoevski*

1. Lighten Up and Live, or Tighten Up and Leave

THE need to lighten up and remain creative under pressure is often, oddly enough, illuminated by tragedy. If you think you've had a bad day at the office, and humor is irrelevant to your problems, the story of Flight 232 may change your mind.

On a Wing, a Prayer, and a Sense of Humor

On a July afternoon in 1989, Captain Alfred Haynes, a thirty-three-year veteran of United Airlines, was in command of a DC-10 lifting off into the clear skies above Denver's Stapleton Airport. As the plane rose steadily on its flight path toward Chicago, it banked into a wide, even turn, giving Haynes and many of the 296 passengers a spectacular view of the Rocky Mountains shimmering gray and emerald green in the unusually clear, smog-free skies.

One hour later, as the aircraft cruised at 37,000 feet, the rear engine exploded. Forty-one terrifying minutes later, the disabled jet crashed in a ball of fire and smoke as the pilot attempted an emergency landing at a small airport in Sioux City, Iowa.

When I saw the videotape of that accident played over and over again on the news, I thought of how often I had been on that same flight, which was a common one for me to take east on business. Later, I discovered that two people I had known died in that crash.

The tragedy of Flight 232 is that 111 people died. The miracle is that 185 people survived . . . in an aircraft which aeronautical experts agreed *could not* be flown.

The engine explosion had wiped out the hydraulic system that allows the pilot to control the flaps and steer the plane. Still, Al Haynes, with the assistance of a training instructor who happened to be on board, found a way to maneuver the plane by using engine thrust alone—a technique called dolphining—to keep the aircraft aloft long enough to attempt the emergency landing.

I think it is safe to assume that, as the captain sat in that cockpit trying to coax his machine to stay in the air, he was not worrying about the effectiveness of his deodorant, or whether or not now was the time to refinance his home. I think it is safe to assume that this was the most terrifying, demanding, and focused experience in his life. Handed a hopeless situation, with all the odds suggesting that he truly was about to die, he still had to take care of a few problems. This was crunch time, when the serious business of training and experience would come through to save the day . . . or it wouldn't. All the captain had to do was perform an unbelievably complex technical procedure that no one had ever before accomplished, while seated in the nose of a crippled airplane which was about to crash . . . and just maybe he and some of the three hundred people depending on him for their lives might have some chance of surviving.

Sound a bit tense? Sound like the time to get "*really serious*"?

Well, here's a snippet of conversation between Captain Haynes and the Sioux City air-traffic control that took place in the final seconds of approach.

Bachman: If you cannot make the airport, sir, there is an interstate that runs . . . to the east side of the airport.

Haynes: We're just passing it right now. We're going to try for the airport.

Bachman: You're cleared to land on any runway.

Haynes (laughing): Roger. You want to be particular and make it a *runway*, huh?

Alan Alda, John Wayne, and Princess Leia

If there's a familiar ring to that story of the heroic airline pilot, cracking a one-liner to keep cool under pressure, it's because humor in the real moment of crisis probably dates back to Moses. It certainly dates back as far as Hollywood can remember. We've always seen our screen heroes and heroines look into the abyss and shrug it off with a joke. Katharine Hepburn and Humphrey Bogart faced the bad guys and the tough times with a curl to the lip, a glimmer in the eye, and a punch line to the funny bone. The television series *M*A*S*H* went on for at least a decade about the power of humor to keep people sane and effective under the extreme pressures of wartime madness.

We admire the heroic calm of a Captain Haynes, the spunky one-liners of Princess Leia in *Star Wars*, and Hawkeye's rebellious humor. And even in our own, considerably less dramatic lives, we've probably all seen a well-timed infusion of comedy break the tension in a family or business crisis, defuse an ugly scene, motivate the troops and get people going again when panic and dread are just about to make them completely numb-brained and dysfunctional.

We may even know full well why laughter feels so good as it does so much good—all the physiological and biochemical reasons why a belly laugh works just like a drug to immediately lower blood pressure, ease the nervous stomach, and free up the mind for creative problem solving—not when it's Miller time, but right there while the kitchen's still in flames, and the lay-offs at work are getting closer to your door every day . . . but frankly just at the moment we've got the third quarter budget to reforecast and the kids to pick up at the dentist and Mom's just been taken to the hospital for tests and our marriage counselor is getting a divorce and things are just a little too serious right now to think about the survival value of humor. OKAY!

That's what the comic strip character Mr. Boffo calls "failure to grasp the concept." I understand. The day-to-day problems of the world kept me from developing the true resilience of humor for most of my life.

If we've seen the benefit of keeping things light under dramatic, life-and-death pressure and we know it's a good idea, why *do* we tune out the message just when we need it most? Why do we tighten up, instead of lighten up, at the first sign of our own day-to-day troubles? Why does routine conflict sometimes make us so brittle that our first response to difficulty is to place blame and drop-kick the dog out the door? And why do we carry our problems like assorted albatrosses around our necks when the most effective way to find solutions is with a fresh perspective and a relaxed, free-flowing imagination?

The answer—and the point of this book—is that the humor which gives us "grace under pressure" isn't some cosmic quirk but rather a set of specific, learned skills. And just as in any other discipline, before we experience the benefit, the skills need to be developed.

Humor can help you thrive in change, remain creative under pressure, work more effectively, play more enthusiastically, and stay healthier in the process. But the skills have to be practiced until they're a habit, a part of your routine. Only then can the resilience and creative flexibility they provide be right there, ready and available when *your* equivalent of the DC-10 blows an engine.

Humor is a set of skills, but it is also an outlook on the world. For the lucky few who were raised with a lifetime of love and support and warmth (which I sometimes think is limited to Andy Hardy, the Muppets, and those kids on *Father Knows Best*), this is as easy as flunking calculus. For the rest of us . . . well, we could use a little help now and then, and that's what this book aims to provide.

Lighten Up is based on the absurdly successful seminars I've been giving to businesses and other groups around the world for the past ten years. Part of it deals with attitudes and outlook, some of it addresses the etiquette of humor and the pitfalls to avoid when using humor in dealing with others, but most of it is designed to teach you specific techniques you can use to put humor to work as a survival skill in your everyday life, right there in the privacy of your own home or surrounded by your fellow dweebs down at the office.

Which is not to say that this is a book about telling jokes.

Jokes are a form of humor, and joke telling makes one a comic, and comedy is the art form of humor . . . but I wouldn't advise it as a career choice. My observation is that only about 2 percent of the population is capable of remembering and telling jokes anyway, which is why Bill Cosby is a millionaire and we're still making payments.

For the 98 percent of us who can't tell jokes—or, who think we can only when honest friends are absent—humor is a way of seeing, salving, and solving the serious issues of our lives, and that's the humor we're talking about. But even here, humor and laughter do not exist in the absence of sorrow and tears, they co-exist as a balance of sanity.

Friedrich Nietzsche, that philosophical wild and crazy guy, observed: "The most acutely suffering animal on earth invented laughter." Suffering and silliness are interwoven here because, as in the Captain Haynes story, and so many others in this book, the value of humor is best reflected when people confront crisis.

WHEN I first became aware that humor could serve as a survival tool, I spent a lot of time feeling inadequate because other people found it seemingly so easy to lighten up. It was difficult for me to believe I could, or even should, lighten up because I'd spent most of my life hiding a dead serious attitude behind a phony grin. As a confused child from an alcoholic family, I learned early that life could be cold and unpredictable, the world a place where only the tough—and, at times, the entertaining—survived. I was suspicious of people who were laughing and having a good time. Before I learned these skills, I thought that such people were dingbats; I was sure that if they really understood how painful life was, they wouldn't be laughing.

Many of us who had to struggle against the odds were lucky just to crawl into adulthood with some semblance of sanity. But we did the right thing, you know—we survived.

Now it may be that what we need to do most is to learn to laugh a little more, to take ourselves—even our pain—a bit less seriously. In time, we might even learn how the humor skills I want to teach you can take the bitterness out of our failings, and make our success that much sweeter.

But there's another reason why it's so easy for us to abandon humor just when we need it, and why we choose, instead, to become slathering beasts that berated subordinates and terrify small children: We've been raised in a culture that believes our problems can be beaten only if we just get tough enough, work a little harder, and get really serious!

The Protestant work ethic so dear to our blood pressure arrived on the East Coast with the Puritans about 400 years ago and caught the first oxcart west. Long hours behind the plow and the covered wagon moved us ever closer to Portland and L.A., while the six-gun and repeating rifle were eliminating those who disagreed with us or stood in the way. Blood, sweat, and tears built factories, railroads, and the city of Milwaukee.

In a material sense—at least for a small "in" crowd—this grit-your-teeth attitude brought us great prosperity. But then in the middle of our own pleasant little century, as life became increasingly complex and the cost–benefit ratio between work and reward tilted not necessarily in our favor, stress was fingered by the medical profession as an enemy that could kill.

Several decades later, now, we're working harder than ever, but—is it any surprise?—still falling behind. We have a tradition to be maintained, one that taught us we could outwork, outsmart, and outgun any threat, be it the tyranny of European kings, an unmapped continent, bad guys in black hats, poverty, social ills, or global competition.

Our cultural obsession with success and winning really went through the roof in the eighties, when men and women everywhere strapped on their briefcases, put their shoulders to the wheel, wiped those stupid smiles off their faces, and got lean, mean, and serious. Dead serious. We set aside such "frivolous" indulgences as family, joy, and laughter, in favor of trying to outgun and outwork ever-increasing levels of change and stress. My God, if we did play, we couldn't feel good about it unless it was aerobic, honed our competitive skills, or allowed us to do business at the same time. Yes sir, we even learned to "play hard." Doesn't that sound like fun? We couldn't even allow ourselves to lighten up when we were covered with sweat in our goofy-looking jogging outfits!

And what are the results of this pedal-to-the-metal, kick-it-in, get-serious, work-harder-at-everything-including playtime, approach? One is a deadly effect on our work. The other is a deadly effect on us.

Stressed for Excess

Much of the research mentioned throughout this book supports what I have noticed in my life and in the lives of others: silliness in the face of seriousness is a mark of mental health, and the failure to find humor in threatening situations can indicate dullness, rigidity, and sometimes even mental illness.

In *Taking Laughter Seriously,* philosopher John Morreall explains why it works this way. He tells us that "the person who has a sense of humor is not just more relaxed in the face of potentially stressful situations, but is more flexible in his approach. Even when there is not a lot going on in his environment, his imagination and innovativeness will help keep him out of a mental rut, will allow him to enjoy himself, and so will prevent boredom and depression."

I don't know if philosopher Morreall reads Latin, but I'll bet he knows that the root of the word humor is *umor* . . . which means fluid, like water. (Latin's a snap—you just drop the first letter.)

Humor, then, is a set of survival skills that relieve tension, keeping us fluid and flexible instead of allowing us to become rigid and breakable, in the face of relentless change.

IN spring 1991 I attended a conference at which author Edward de Bono, who may be the world's leading authority on creativity, explained that **humor and the creative process are actually one and the same thing.** With both forms of thinking—humor and general creativity—he said, the brain recognizes the value of the absurdity or the creative idea only in hindsight. Prior to that moment, both innovation and humor seem "crazy." But it is the willingness to *play* with ideas, to *risk* foolishness without fear, that are the hallmarks of creative thinkers. And it is the creativity which springs from humor that increases our effectiveness. After surveying 382 people from diverse occupations, David Abramis, a psychologist at California State University at Long Beach, concluded "that those who felt their work was *fun* performed better and got along better with coworkers than did those who were satisfied with their jobs but did not see them as fun." Dr. Alice M. Isen, of the Department of Psychology and Johnson Graduate School of Management at Cornell University, did an even niftier study and found that even people who had just seen a funny movie had a "creative flexibility" greatly expanded over those who had not. The subjects who were denied a humor dose before problem assignments suffered from what she called "functional fixedness." (Which must be the academic label for being stuck.)

I often cite studies like these when I'm trying to convince some manager that the radical idea of humor in the workplace will increase, rather than decrease, creativity and productivity.

When I was first hired to offer this material in corporate environments, I was amazed at how many people still believed that *If you're having fun, it can't be work, because why else would they call it work?* In their minds—work has to hurt.

Laughter—the Cheapest Medicine

When Norman Cousins began investigating humor in the 1970s, he uncovered the key supporting proofs that positive emotional states enhance physical and

psychological healing. Cousins's *Head First: The Biology of Hope,* published not long before his death
in 1991, should be required reading for the cynic,
grump, or scientist who needs reams of supportive
studies before feeling justified in pursuing humor as
a rational, intelligent, and worthwhile pastime.

One of the most significant of the discoveries Cousins reports is that sustained laughter stimulates an
increased release of endorphins—the body's own, natural morphine. **We feel better when we laugh, because
endorphins actually diminish physical *and* psychological pain.** Subsequent findings that endorphins
also stimulate the body's immune system to increase
its disease-fighting ability, make laughter—if not the
best—certainly the cheapest medicine we can get over
or under the counter.

Endorphin studies help to explain another phenomenon that interests me. In my research I found that
laughter was considered a healthy sign of recovery
among drug addicts and alcoholics. Now I know why.
Psychologically, they are laughing at what used to terrify them, and that indicates an increasing sense of
inner control and perspective. But that same laughter
is pumping up endorphins—*morphine,* for crying out
loud!

This is your brain—[picture of an egg]
This is your brain on Laughter. [picture of a dancing,
rubber chicken]

OTHER studies cited in *Head First* show the range of
humor's beneficial consequences. Dr. William Fry, Jr., of
the Department of Psychiatry at Stanford Medical
School, contends that laughter is a natural and invaluable means for strengthening the heart muscle. Addi-

tional research has shown that sustained, frequent laughter also helps some people to lower blood pressure. Dr. Fry's work has shown that just twenty seconds of laughter is the cardiovascular equivalent of three minutes of strenuous rowing. And yes, I think this does mean there's a niche market for "Happy Health" clubs where, instead of those washboard-tummy, glistening types who make you want to go home and shoot yourself, the instructors will be potbellied clowns and comics.

Dr. Gary E. Schwartz of the Yale University Department of Psychology actually found that when people who were angry or sad engaged in exercise, their biochemical and cardiovascular benefits were diminished. Exercising in a positive and relaxed context allowed the participants in Dr. Schwartz's study to increase the health benefits of their workout by as much as one-half.

ARTHUR Koestler (a great novelist, but not a man known for his zany sense of humor), wrote that "laughter is a reflex but unique in that it has no apparent biological purpose. One might call it a luxury reflex. **Its only function seems to be to provide relief from tension.**"

Only relief from tension, you say? I don't know how you spell relief, Art, but when it's free, nonalcoholic, and singularly devoid of a downside, I take it as a gift.

Some people use exercise to try to get that relief; we know others turn to alcohol and drugs. The irony is that when carried to an extreme, such attempts create devastating side effects that are more stressful than the worries they are trying to eliminate.

Exercise and meditation are excellent self-management tools, but these techniques offer little immediate help when the dive-bombers of change are strafing the decks. Hopping up in the middle of a business meeting to slam a few rounds of handball off the office wall is generally considered inappropriate. Going into a meditative trance while negotiating rush-hour traffic is also ill-advised.

With humor skills, though, you can lighten up as you lie in a hospital bed, stand in an elevator, or, ideally, wait an hour in the express checkout line at the grocery store behind the guy with forty-seven items. You have instant access to a miracle drug with immediate effects that doesn't cost you a cent or require any heavy lifting.

Getting Serious About Silliness

By choosing to develop our capacity for humor, fun, and laughter we exert a direct, biochemical effect on our overall wellness by making our fears manageable and sustaining our hopes. But because humor skills often show up when people face their worst difficulties, I have learned most of the lessons in this book from people who have known as much about sorrow as about joy.

One of the first steps in my own "education" occurred in 1978, when I encountered a group of terminally ill children at the Center for Attitudinal Healing in Tiburon, California. They convinced me that humor could be learned and successfully applied to even the most awful situations.

The time I spent with those kids was the beginning of learning how to lighten up and enjoy the trip, no matter what the terrain might offer. Despite their fear, despite their illness, the children at the Center knew the meaning of *umor*. By staying loose, they managed to keep sight of humor, hope, and laughter. There were times when the kids were in pain, when they were sad, when they cried. But their tears were balanced by insistence on looking for the things in life that brought them joy.

One of my greatest inspirations was a thirteen-year-old girl I'll call Lindy, who secretly taped a note to her tummy for the doctor to find in the operating room. It said:

> While you're taking out my tumor, please remove the mole on my nose. I'm going to be a movie star, and that thing has just got to go. See you soon.

In this book I'm not going to suggest that you abdicate responsibility for your difficulties and become a dipstick Pollyanna whistling, "Don't Worry, Be Happy." Quite the opposite. But I do suggest that we quit focusing on the idiocy of others and the cruel circumstances of a universe that seems, at times, to be conspiring against us. The goal here is to find all the answers that we can within ourselves. And more than anything else, what we need to find in there is *umor*, the fluidity and flexibility of water. Water wears granite into sand. *Umor* allows us to flow through difficulties instead of being broken by them. As water brings life to any environment, humor nurtures life and makes it worth the effort.

A Serious Note . . .

I'm not a doctor. I don't even play one on television, but my understanding of humor as skills— not jokes—saved my life. Maybe it can do the same for you.

Although *Lighten Up* offers the latest medical and psychological research on the value of humor, it draws heavily upon my own experiences and those of my worldwide client base. Part of the prescription has to do with adopting attitudes that will help you thrive in change and crisis. Another element has to do with specific techniques that bring humor into your life just when you really need it.

Although *Lighten Up* offers serious solutions to twenty-first-century stresses, some should exercise caution, because primary blocks to humor skill development have to be addressed before this book can be of much use.

If you are or have been a victim of sexual abuse, if you don't know whether or not your spouse will beat you up, if you can't control your own violent temper, there's no laughing it off.

Before I could begin to lighten up, I had to overcome my own major block to understanding the value of humor—alcoholism. You may not have that or any other problem. There may be nothing at all between you and the ability to lighten up. But, just in case . . .

Lighten Up addresses the most common issues of denial that might stand in the way of your developing humor skills. If you get depressed easily, you might read Chapter 10 before going any further. If, like me, you've suffered from "abusive" humor such as teasing or sexism or racism, try Chapter 8. If you have a problem with drugs or alcohol, read Chapter 9.

If the suggestions in this book don't take you as far as you want to go, or perhaps bring up unpleasant associations, set it aside and, as Dr. Ruth so often advises, "Zee a goot terapist." We want to help you, not to make you feel uncomfortable.

There comes a time . . . when we must grab
the bull by the tail and face the situation.
—W. C. Fields

2. Learning It the Hard Way

I HAVE no argument with hard work, brains, talent, a solid sense of values—even a great education, loads of charm, and fabulous connections. I recommend these goodies to everyone I meet . . . but there's not much I can do to help you get them.

And frankly, I don't think that's where the problem lies for most of us, or that any of those virtues are the simple solution to managing one's life and finding happiness. To tell you the absolute truth, I think a critical factor that explains why some people solve their problems and others collapse under their weight has a lot more to do with—nah . . . let me guess— their sense of humor.

Sound stupid to you? Then let me explain the kind of humor I'm talking about. The best way to do that is to lay out for you the three humor skills. These are the basics I hope you'll come away with after reading this book.

The First Humor Skill: The ability to see the absurdity in difficult situations.

The Second Humor Skill: The ability to take yourself lightly while taking your work seriously.

The Third Humor Skill: A disciplined sense of joy in being alive.

That's how you get the fluidity, creativity, and flexibility I'm here trying to sell—by mastering those three little skills.

Which is not as easy as you might think. It's taken me a lifetime to learn what I've just shrunk down into six lines of copy. But with any luck, this book might just speed up the learning for you.

By the time I stumbled on the need for humor skills *in my life,* I was already in my thirties. What's more, I'd been working as a comedy writer—which is one of life's cuter ironies.

This whole business began for me on a particularly wet spring day in 1978. At that time in my history, the only aspect of "fluidity" I understood was the buckets of rainwater pouring down on my convertible as I drove north on California highway 101 toward the city of Tiburon.

After three major career changes (none of which I had been consulted about or agreed to) and three divorces (the most recent ending when my career as a performing mime and my third marriage simultaneously disintegrated), I had only the darkest doubts about my future. Other guys my age were trading their Hondas in on Volvo station wagons, moaning about the IRS and the demise of tax shelters. Me? I was scrambling to pay the rent on a rundown converted garage in Los Angeles, shopping generic, and pretending that accumulated cases of cheap wine made me a connoisseur.

Recently, though, I had landed steady work as a scriptwriter and actor for children's television, a career that tied in with my theory of trusting no one over seven. Of course I was *dead serious* about comedy and this job. But despite a stunning performance as Drucko the clown on *Happy Days*; an appearance with Betty Thomas (later a star of *Hill Street Blues*) wherein we offered a memorable portrayal of two potato chips in turmoil; and intermittent writing and acting for children's television, I had failed to capture much of Hollywood's imagination or cash.

The rain intensified as I downshifted my shuddering MGB and continued on toward the Bay Area. My writing partner, Harvey Brenner, stared attentively at the crossword puzzle that rested on one raised knee. His paunchy frame was crammed into the tiny leather passenger seat.

"M-m-m-m-m, lessee, five letters for minnow stalker: Heron? Stork? Egret? Egret. That's it," he exclaimed. "Unable to attend your aquarium opening, I send my egrets."

I groaned. Harvey seemed to revel in making me cringe. He reveled a lot.

I cranked up the radio and considered the script Harvey and I planned to write about the children we were on our way to see. A little more than a week ago, I had learned about these kids the way *real* Americans so often learn things—by watching the *Donahue* show.

That morning, as I studied the screen from the sofa in my apartment, Phil had been interviewing a psychiatrist named Jerry Jampolsky and a group of children

from a place called the Center for Attitudinal Healing
in Tiburon, California. Not a surprise, I thought. With
a name like that, the place would have to be in California. The children had created and published a book,
There Is a Rainbow Behind Every Dark Cloud.

I had been on the verge of switching stations, but
before I could put together the complex chain of decisions necessary to rise from the couch, move six feet,
and turn the dial, Phil zeroed in on a boy about ten
years old. The child had a Spanish surname, dark hair
that fell across his forehead, almost covering his eyes,
and an ivory-toothed grin.

Phil paced off with his elbow-flapping impression of
a gull about to take flight. "Here you are, so young,
with cancer. I mean, a disease that—you know—
might lead to your, well, gee, *to your death,* in a very
short while. But you seem happy. I don't get it!" Flap-
flap. "It seems so . . . *unfair.*"

As I watched the screen from the couch, I silently
agreed, and I felt Phil's audience agree, too. Here was
further proof—as if I needed it—that the universe
was cruel and unforgiving.

The boy cocked his head slightly to one side. "Well,
gee," he began with that wry grin—was he mimicking
Phil?—"my life is more than having cancer, you
know. At the Center, we help each other, and I guess
that keeps us from feeling too sorry for ourselves."

Phil held the microphone close to his lips. "*But*
if I were in your situation I'd be, well, I don't know,
but I think I'd be *really* scared! How can you be so
brave?"

The child cracked a smile. "Calm down, will ya. I
don't know why *you're* so upset. *I'm* the one who's
sick."

Phil and the audience hesitated, then, suddenly, as if everyone had received permission at the same moment, they all laughed too.

But I couldn't.

Here was a child whose one problem made all mine seem about as significant as a case of razor burn, yet he was happy and I was miserable. If the kid was for real—and not a child actor reciting lines from a script, or on drugs, or under the influence of some bizarre guru—he clearly knew *something* about life and happiness that I didn't.

Now, as I pulled into an apparently infinite line of cars entering Pacific Palisades, I was forced to slow the MGB to a crawl. To the west, and just below the sound of the rain, we heard the soft roar of ocean surf. Harvey's round face rose from its focus on the puzzle book. He looked at me with that squinty-eyed, goofy grin that changed him from Buddha to Bozo. "You ought to have a Volkswagen for this trip, C.W."

"How come?"

"They float."

The Rainbow Gang

We parked the car on Main Street in Tiburon and followed the signs to the Center. Dr. Jampolsky's office was in a small gray and white building on a landing that reached out over the bay. "Harvey? C.W.?" Jerry Jampolsky came striding toward us from his office. His mostly gray hair was cut short, and he wore a sportcoat, slacks, and tie.

Following the obligatory small talk, Jerry shepherded us into the Center, which was next door to his office in a separate, much larger building. He

introduced us to several of the volunteers, then he
showed us around. Several tiny rooms were cluttered
with files, and the walls were covered by pictures
drawn by the kids. One room was lined with pillows
and chairs. "We have weekly group meetings here," he told us.
"The children, their parents, friends, teachers, siblings—whoever the kids want to invite."

Next, he pointed out a set of shelves crammed with
books, pamphlets, and papers. "This is the beginning
of our reference library. And some copies of the book
the children wrote." He handed us two oversized copies of *There Is a Rainbow Behind Every Dark Cloud.*
"Here, one for each of you," he said. On the cover, a
drawing showed two children looking up into the
sky, where a bright rainbow cut through the black
clouds.

After a few meetings with volunteers, we walked
back across the deck to Jerry's office. The view was a
real-estate dealer's dream.

"I have one main reservation about your project,"
he told us. "It's critical that we avoid making the children feel as though they'll be famous *because* they
have cancer. All the media exposure lately has created
some problems. These kids are beautiful teachers, but
they are children, so be considerate."

"What do you mean?" Harvey asked.

"Well," Jerry said, "most people have strong opinions about what we're doing here. To some, attitudinal
healing gives new hope for dealing with cancer, illness, and distress in general; for others, it's a sham, a
delusion, a support of false hope that only makes people's lives more difficult. Depending on your point of
view, you might be tempted to ask leading questions

to get what you're looking for. All I ask is that you respect these children and their families."

"Clear enough," Harvey said.

I wasn't as clear about it as Harvey seemed to be, but I nodded sagely and said something deeply philosophical, like "Uh huh."

THE Center had been founded in 1976 as a six-week experiment that would explore new ways of helping catastrophically ill children. Chemotherapy and radiation treatments were combined with newer approaches, including biofeedback and guided imagery.

But the most controversial aspect of treatment was this *attitudinal healing*, a philosophy described in the book, *A Course in Miracles*. With this approach, kids were taught that there were only two emotions: love and fear. They believed it was possible to choose *happiness* even when they were sick, to forgive the past and help each other.

Surrounded as I was by this happy "Rainbow Gang" of courageous people who spent far more time enjoying themselves and feeling good than I ever had, I could see there was something to this approach.

After four days in Tiburon, Harvey had to return to L.A. to deal with what seemed like a semimonthly family crisis. Earlier, though, we had accepted an invitation to join the kids, volunteers, families, and friends at a Family Day celebration at Jerry's home, and so I went on alone.

I was already in a "mood" from having trouble finding a place to park, but as soon as I got to the door I heard laughter, chatter, and sporadic shrieks. The living room, dining room, kitchen, and deck were spilling over with people, including ten kids, somewhere between ages six and fourteen. The rest of the group consisted of older teens and some of the parents I had talked with earlier.

A few of the children were so thin I would have sworn that sunlight would pass through them making no shadow. Some had lost hair to radiation and chemotherapy. I recognized three of the older children. One of them, a girl, noticed me and rushed over to where I stood sipping white wine and plotting my strategy.

"Hey, neat, you're doing a movie, maybe? I don't want to star in it or anything, but I want to learn about writing, okay? Will you teach me? I'm gonna be a writer, too, you know. When's the movie coming out?"

I tried to explain that it wasn't a movie, but a television special, and that it wasn't definite.

"Of course it's not definite," she chattered on, as she followed me toward the kitchen. "Nothing is ever really definite, is it? I mean, if you don't know what's gonna happen, though, why not expect the best?"

To avoid disappointment, I replied in my thoughts, but what I said was, "What do you mean?"

Jerry interrupted before the child could answer. "C.W.! Come over here and meet someone."

I spent the next hour in a buzz of conversation that I don't recall clearly. I played pantomime games with the kids, conducted interviews, and generally tried to look pleasant and attentive.

Finally, I went outside to the deck to smoke a guilt-laced cigarette. The sky had clouded over and the light rain that San Franciscans call "fog" had settled in.

Maybe I wasn't capable of understanding these people or the way they thought about things, it occurred

to me. Or maybe all of them were just plain crazy. I
began to consider wrapping up early so that I could
get home quickly to my life in L.A.

At that precise moment, I felt a tugging on my
jacket. One of the little kids, about seven or eight,
stood next to me. He was hairless—not an eyebrow,
an eyelash—no strand grew from his face or head. He
was thin, and the "fog" drizzled down his little bald
crown like water off an egg. He was smiling.

"How are you?" I asked.

"I'm fine, C.W." But then for a moment he looked
uneasy, as if he were trying to figure the best way of
saying something difficult. "Well, but I was wondering . . . You don't look so good. You want to come in
and sit down?"

I rolled my eyes up into my head. He wants me to *sit
down*? And what does he mean, I don't look so good?
My God, this kid with cancer, this kid who's obviously
lost all his hair to chemotherapy, is worried about
me? He thought *I* didn't look so good?

"Do you hurt much?" he asked.

At the time I didn't get it, but later I realized that,
because I was bald, the boy thought I too must be going through chemo. At that moment, all I knew was
that this small, frail child, with the biggest, bluest
eyes I'd ever been trapped in, had stepped outside
himself enough to recognize my pain. But how could
it be so obvious? How could he, in the face of his own
crisis, express concern for me? His compassion cut
through my defenses like a scalpel. I realized that
tears were running down my face.

"It's okay," he said, nodding. "I was scared in the
beginning, too. It's good to cry when you feel like it.
But it helps if you talk about it, too. That's how you let

go of things, or part of it, anyway." He nodded toward the house. "If you want to talk to me or my folks, we're in there by the fireplace."

It was all I could do to light another cigarette as I muttered some vague kind of "thank you." My hands shook. My chest hurt.

"We're here to help each other," he said, "so, lighten up." Then, just before going inside, he reached up with a tiny hand and patted me on the small of the back.

I turned toward the ocean and let it rip. The tears washed down my face like that rain on the Coast road. I *was* sick—the kid had been on the money about that, but what was *wrong* with me?

And lighten up? Sure. Fine. Of course. But how do you *do* that?

By about 8:30 P.M., all the guests had left. I thanked Jerry and told him that I'd decided to go back to L.A. in the morning. I started toward the guest bedroom. "Got to get organized," I told him.

"No problem," Jerry came back. But then, after a pause, "C.W.—Did you learn anything from the kids?"

"Oh, yeah," I said, "You bet."

He waited for me to explain.

"I can't talk about it now, Jerry," was all I could say.

AT about that time, a professor of psychiatry at Harvard Medical School named George Vaillant, who had analyzed the results of a forty-year study of healthy young men, published his findings in the book *Adaptation to Life*. One of Dr. Vaillant's primary observations was that healthy people were not those who experienced less stress, but rather, people who used

mature methods to cope effectively with the problems
they encountered.

From cancer patients like the kids in Tiburon, to
hostages in the Middle East, to Holocaust survivors—
from stressed-out corporate Superwomen, angst-filled
teens, and exhausted house husbands, people who en-
dure stress without becoming brittle, bitter, and broken have several traits in common:

- **They are altruistic, *actively caring about the wel-
  fare of others.*** A friend of mine explained that the
  difference between martyrdom and altruism is that
  the genuine altruist always gives from the *over-
  flow* of his or her energy, and not from the core.
  When people operating under the banner of martyrdom finish "helping people," they feel resent-
  ful and exhausted. The altruist invariably feels
  better.

- **Humor.** Dr. Vaillant's definition of humor was not
  jokes or the talent to do stand-up comedy, but the
  ability to see the absurdity in our greatest fears.
  Successful people used a humor perspective to
  gain control of difficult situations and to maintain a sense of joy in the journey of being alive.
  They took time to play and built the discipline to
  take themselves lightly while taking their jobs,
  problems, or challenges seriously.

- **They draw support from friends and community.**
  The study showed that healthy, long-lived people
  form close, lasting friendships that act as a cush-
  ion against trauma and difficulty. Both altruism
  and humor, healthy defenses in themselves, also
  enhance this social support. I had always worried

that close attachments would suck the life out of me. Apparently, healthy people manage to form attachments without becoming so dependent on the group that they lose their individuality.

Dying to Feel Good

More than anything else at the Center for Attitudinal Healing, the children's ability to minimize their own fear and pain by focusing on service to others inspired and confused me. Those young people had been so intent on helping others, they managed to persuade the phone company to install a free worldwide line into the Center so that terminally ill kids could call from anywhere and talk to other patients their age. (I considered getting a free *anything* from the phone company something of a miracle.)

During my initial interviews with Jampolsky, I had suggested that it must feel good to know he was doing so much for the kids.

He laughed. "It's unfair to say that I have helped these children. The truth is that anything I've done for them or their families has been returned to me a thousandfold."

It had sounded hokey at the time, but there they were: children with cancer, their families, volunteers, and Jerry, all helping one another and all able to experience more joy, humor, and laughter than I, a supposedly healthy man of thirty-three, could imagine.

I made my mind up that night to work with cancer patients to try to understand what the kids seemed to know already. By God, I thought, if giving and sharing is what it takes to become happy, joyous, and free of the ravages of my life, then I'd jump in and start to give. I'd give until it hurt, until I got what I wanted, until it killed me if necessary!

When I returned to L.A., I signed up for a hospice training program. I wanted to be fearless—to feel as good, spiritually and emotionally, as the people at the Center. Besides, Harvey agreed that my participation in an actual hospice training experience would help us add authenticity to the script we were working on.

THE training course was scheduled for twelve weeks of evening and weekend sessions that covered everything, from the history of the hospice movement to such topics as grief counseling and changing bedpans. Afterward, we would be ready for assignment by the local hospice director to work as volunteers with terminally ill patients. We would drive clients to appointments, pick up their medications, and help out with day-to-day needs.

Most important, we would listen. Our instructors had told us that one of the most difficult things for hospice patients to cope with is loneliness. Apparently, no matter how many books, films, or television shows about death people have encountered, they come to understand the true meaning of their mortality only upon confronting it. At that border, the patient feels unique. Hospice provides him or her with a partner who understands the value of human dignity—who can help the patient to escape the often self-imposed isolation.

As the program continued, we were presented with a variety of instructors: physicians, nurses, social workers, psychologists, experienced hospice volunteers, even patients who were living with cancer, or who had experienced remission. But by the sixth week all the class work, lectures, readings, and role playing had started to make me edgy.

After a session entitled, "Active Listening," which was almost impossible for me to concentrate on, I invited the instructor out to dinner. Louise was a retired RN who had been doing hospice volunteer work for several years. I was impressed with how easily she laughed and the stories she told about her clients, or "teachers," as she called them.

"Remember," she told the class, "whether your clients deal with their illness in a rage, a hostile silence, a state of peace or agitation, they know more about what they feel than you do. Learn from them. Most often, you'll feel stronger when you leave them. If not, you're missing the point."

Through dinner and dessert, I stressed how eager I was to get to work. Louise had not seemed impressed. Instead, she smiled in that odd way she had, eyes half closing as the corners of her mouth curled slightly up. By the time coffee arrived, I must have sounded desperate. "I need to do this work," I told her. "It's important."

With the fingertips of one parchment-smooth hand, she tucked a strand of silver hair behind the earpiece of her glasses. "I'm not sure you know what you're getting into," she said quietly. "But you'll find out soon enough. We all do."

"I can help out as an aide," I insisted. "We can use my car. It'll be a sort of on-the-job training experience."

Despite her apparent skepticism, Louise had allowed me to work with her when she visited a patient, a man of seventy-six with colon cancer that had spread throughout his body. In less than five months, his weight had gone from around two hundred pounds to just under one hundred. The skin was shrunken so tightly over his bald skull that, except for the large, bright brown eyes and massive growths of hair in his ears, Ed looked like a skeleton. After months in and out of hospitals and the removal of so many internal parts that, in his words, "They could make another old fart out of the pieces they've taken out of me," he decided to cease all attempts to extend his life and die as peacefully as possible in his own home.

"Ah," he said when we first met, "someone who's as bald as I am! We should be able to relate."

But after only a few visits, Ed began to grumble about my "attitude." I wrote off his complaints as the sour vision of a dying old man, but it bothered me when he grouched, just loudly enough for me to hear, about what a wet blanket I was, or how I never laughed at his jokes, which he said were "damned funny, by God. They've been funny for fifty frickin' years, and they're still funny."

Louise handled Ed's primary care, but I was allowed to assist. I was giving; I was caring; I was helpful. I even entertained Ed with mime pieces and comic bits.

Why then wasn't I happy? Even more difficult to understand, why didn't he like me?

One afternoon, when Louise had left Ed and me together while she went out to pick up supplies and prescriptions for him, I sat next to his bed in a darkened room and watched him sleep. The bare outline of his body under the blankets seemed much too small for the large head that rested on the pillow. His eyes were

closed and his breath rasped in and out as though his
lungs resented the job. Without opening his eyes or
moving a single unnecessary muscle, he whispered
his often-repeated question:

"Well, boy, you ready for the long march to the
toilet?"

I crossed to the bed and peeled back the covers. His
thin body was draped in his favorite Mickey Mouse
pajamas. I helped him, very slowly, to sit up, bring
his legs over the edge of the mattress, put on his slip-
pers, and rise to his feet. His wispy arm around my
back, his huge, bony hand resting on my shoulder, we
started our slow, shuffling walk to the bathroom. It
usually took us about ten minutes to reach our desti-
nation, with several breathing stops along the way.

There was a wheelchair to use for moving Ed
around, but he called it his *banshee wagon* and said,
"The only time I'll get in that frickin' thing is when
they wheel me out dead. If I can walk, I'm gonna walk.
If I can't walk, I'll just die." And so the glistening new
wheelchair, provided by our hospice office, sat like
some article from a future civilization among Ed's
vintage-1945 living-room collection.

On our return trip from the bathroom, Ed was
breathing hard, and his face was knotted by the effort.
I spoke, trying to distract him from the pain. "You
know, your doctor's coming over later to visit."

"Oh, whoopee," he wheezed.

"Maybe you want me to help you out of those Mickey
Mouse pajamas and into something more respect-
able?"

"I like these p.j.s," he whispered. I helped him sit
down on the edge of his bed. "Mickey reminds me that
I can still laugh a little now and then, which is more

than the frickin' doctor's ever done." Then he muttered, "More 'n you can do for me, too."

I cradled him in my arms and gently allowed his
head to fall back against the pillow while I raised his
legs onto the bed. I was trying to ignore the comment.
"In fact," Ed said, "maybe you should go out and
get some p.j.s with Goofy on 'em. I liked those too, but
I thought these were more in keeping with my advanced years." He started to laugh, then had to restrain himself to keep from choking.

"And," he added, "we could get Louise a Donald
Duck nightshirt, and all meet the doctor singing
'M-I-C, K-E-Y, M-O-U-S-E-eeee . . . ' "

That was too much for him, and he broke into a rat-
tling cough.

As I pulled the covers over him, Ed stopped laughing, looked up at me and shook his head disapprov-
ingly.

"What's the problem, Ed?"

"You, young man. You're the problem."

Knowing that deliriously ill patients sometimes
mistake their caretakers for people they've known in
the past, I played along.

"Well, Ed," I said, smiling, "what have I done this
time?"

"Don't condescend to me, son. Hell, you're worse off
than I am. You know that? In fact, I'd appreciate it if
Louise would find me a volunteer to replace you."

This was the first time he'd come right out and
told me how he felt. I didn't know what to do, so I
laughed.

"It's not funny," Ed said. "Now, listen to me, C.W.,
and pay attention. Every time you come to visit,
you look surprised to see I'm still alive. I don't look

forward to that. I know I'm dyin'. I know I smell like
death, and I get kinda cranky about it sometimes. But
I sure as hell don't need your mournful puss remind-
ing me I look like the ghoul that little kids think is
hidin' in the closet."

He coughed, swallowed with difficulty, and went
on. "I try and try to cheer you up, but you're one of
the most depressing bastards I've ever met. I'd rather
work with someone more positive."

He was making me angry, and sad, and to tell the
truth, afraid.

"Look," I said, "I'm new at this. I'm sorry you don't
like the way I do things, but if you let me know what
you need, I really want to help."

He grinned—at least, I think he grinned. Sometimes, it was hard to tell the difference between his
grins and grimaces.

"I'm tired, C.W. And I just don't have time for this
kind of b.s. I'm sure you're a real nice person, but if
you're here to help, it ain't workin'."

He hesitated.

"You drink too much, ya know? Cripes, I may have
cancer, but I haven't lost my sense of smell yet. Yep,
too much, too early, and too often. God only knows
what else is blockin' you up. When you get it figured
out, come back and visit me."

Naturally, I wanted to argue—to explain that my
drinking was normal. After all, I'd grown up in an
alcoholic household. I knew what problem drinking
really was.

All I could manage to say was, "I see."

There was a wistful smile on Ed's face. "You're here
for *you*, C.W., and I find your company depressing.
Period."

ONE month after I had begun my hospice training in L.A., and six months after my first meeting with Jerry and the kids in Tiburon, I left my work with Ed and finished the hospice program in a halfhearted daze.

On the final day of class, Louise told me that Ed had just died. I'm afraid that the sadness I felt was as much self-pity as it was any sense of loss. Then she rested her hand on my shoulder.

"Ed asked me to give you this," she said. She held up a paper bag with a note attached. "I don't think you knew what you were getting into," she offered quietly. "I hope you'll try again later." Then she wandered off to chat with some other graduates.

I carried the bag, like a time bomb, to my car. Once inside, I placed it on the passenger seat, turned the key in the ignition, then, finally, reached over to unroll the crumpled container. Ed's bequest stared back at me, still wrapped in clear plastic with the price tag in one corner: a T-shirt emblazoned with the grinning, haloed vision of Walt Disney's Goofy. I opened the note:

C.W.
The p.j.s were too worn out to give to you as a going-away present.
Besides, I really want to be buried in
them. Put this shirt on at the first sign that you're taking yourself too seriously. In other words, wear it all the time.   Ed

Now those were the days when spiritual quests were a kind of epidemic, at least for us out in California. I tried est but couldn't hold my bladder long enough to get through the first session. I drifted into even more esoteric and peculiar arenas of spiritual investigation. Oh, I didn't get into chicken sacrifices and voodoo or anything. I liked chickens. I spent time on a farm as a kid where the chickens had names.

I did read every self-help book, consult every guru, stumble down every path from self-hypnosis to fundamentalist Christianity, Buddhism, and Ouija boards and ended up where I'd started: sitting in a bar with a triple rum and tonic, ruminating on my sad history.

Now, fortunately, most people don't have a hurdle as big and complex as alcoholism standing between them and lightening up, but I know from experience that just about everyone has to overcome *something*, even if it is only his or her fear of foolishness. Bear with me a moment while I finish my story, okay?

Through the years, a variety of concerned or appalled people had risked telling me that I had a drinking problem. My response had been, "Yeah, and you're it, so why don't you leave?"

They kept leaving, and I kept drinking. "It figures," I told myself. "If they had my problems, they'd drink, too."

Because it never occurred to me that drinking was the problem I had to solve before anything else could make sense, it would be another two years before I understood what Jerry and the kids at the Center already knew and that I'm now trying to pass along: that humor and joy are skills, not the luck of the draw.

Now, There's the Rub

From the growth of Alcoholics Anonymous and the popularity of various treatment programs, to the candor with which today's celebrities admit they have quit drinking, all indications are that sobriety has become hip. In the early eighties, things weren't that way. People *sneaked* off to recovery programs.

Nothing, including constant threats and advice from friends, wives, employers, judges, and even strangers, had induced me to accept the truth that alcoholism was the primary block to my lightening up and learning to live.

At the Center, I had seen courage, friendship, and fun in an environment I thought should have been hopeless. In the smiles and laughter of children, my alcohol-induced pessimism began to crumble.

But the second event that propelled me toward sobriety was a rather predictable, all things considered, near-death experience. There is something about the prospect of The Big Finish that orders one's priorities and opens the mind. No doubt about it—dying gets your attention.

On this morning it had been raining again for three days and nights. The sky had apparently sucked up great quantities of the Pacific, then burst directly over my house on the north coast of California. I was running low on food but was well stocked with liquor. I had a sinus infection and bronchitis, and was drinking and taking one sleeping pill after another in an attempt to find release in unconsciousness.

All I remember now is having gone into the bathroom. As I stood over the toilet bowl, waiting for my bladder to become aware of its proper function, I suddenly felt lightheaded. I was trying to kneel when something that felt like a hammer of ice slammed into my forehead.

An instant later I felt my "self" floating above the room, staring down at a body clad only in a dirty bathrobe—*my body*, as a matter of fact. A streak of blood smeared the toilet tank where I'd pitched forward and hit my head.

The C.W. on the floor didn't look like much, crumpled in a kneeling position of limp-handed prayer, his head in the bowl, blowing bubbles. I was drowning, in a toilet, but oddly enough it was a moment of profound peace. My floating self was quite euphoric; this miserable, lying, painful life was nearly over, and I figured I was going on to something better.

The cinematic poetry of the moment—the ebbing sensation, the tide pulling me upward, the pure-white light streaming over my shoulders—was tainted by the absurdity of my gurgling, senseless form and bald head bobbing there in the blood-tinged water. It was like *The Lost Weekend* remade by Fellini with the Marx Brothers instead of Ray Milland.

I was going to "let go"—to die—just as soon as I could get my head out of that toilet . . .

But then, I came to, gasping.

Sitting in the middle of the bathroom floor, dripping wet, staring up at the ceiling where I'd been a moment before, I began to laugh. In a moment, in the absurdity of that scene, I saw myself. I finally got it. There *was* a connection between my drinking and my problems. Whether or not I was an alcoholic, I couldn't consider alcohol to be my ally any more. Drinking really had gotten me here, and *here* wasn't pretty.

I muttered prayers of thanks to the kids at the Center, to Jerry, to my misty image of God, to the toilet, to Groucho, Zeppo, Gummo, and Harpo. They had been right: *denial* could kill—at least, I was certain it had the power to kill me.

I laughed until I cried, and cried until I choked, then I crawled into the living room and fell asleep on the couch. I didn't know it, but I had finally set foot on the long and whining road toward learning how to lighten up.

After the Party's Over

I can find some humor in it now, but setting aside the alcohol and drugs that had been my stress-management system for more than twenty years was not fun. It hurt. And I couldn't do it on my own. Like the kids at the Center, I needed group support. After all my bumbling attempts to solve my problems in est, Buddhism, Ouija boards, and mysticism, I sought and found a community of sober alcoholics who helped steer me toward a life without booze, excuses, and self-pity.

In my first year of sobriety I was barely able to think straight, but at least I was walking straight. More important, I became teachable. I was willing to set aside my gloomy world view and risk trying to learn what those kids had tried to teach me: in this life, pain and misery are free; laughter, joy, fun, and humor—the elements that make life worthwhile—take a little effort. But, like so many others who are lovingly attached to their misery, cynicism, and the "harsh realities of the world," I couldn't lighten up by just wanting to. It would take two years of stumbling and grumbling through being sober and clean before the lessons would begin to make sense.

Living, Giving, and Laughing—Together

After my second sobriety birthday, I decided to attempt a reorganization of my life. While rummaging through boxes of old scripts, letters, and magazines, I came across the thick sheaf of notes that Harvey and I had compiled in Tiburon. Alone, sitting cross-legged on my bed, surrounded by hundreds of pages, I began to notice, for the first time, some kind of order, a sort of map that might lead me to the truth of what the Center for Attitudinal Healing was doing for Jerry, the volunteers, the children, and their families. I began to see what those people were doing that I was not.

Anxiously, I began listing the major ideas that seemed to help those kids lighten up and live in the face of such ominous personal crisis and change. After hours of simplifying, only four words remained on the list: **share, care, laugh,** and, at the bottom in parentheses, **(dare).**

As I sat there, wondering exactly what I meant by those words, I would have been intrigued (or do I mean shocked?) to know that two years later, in putting together my first *Humor Option* presentations, I would discover a wealth of modern research that indicated the "simple" concepts I had encountered at the Center were, in fact, part of the "mature" coping skills used by people who thrived in the midst of adversity, change, and crisis.

But Did I Dare?

An understanding of the relation among altruism, humor, and community did not come to me that afternoon. It could have, I suppose, if I had been capable of feeling good at the time. But as a man who had grown up believing that people were untrustworthy, and that humor was more of a weapon for defense or attack, I had a long way to go. Much as I envied the lightheartedness of the volunteers, children, and their families, I still feared it might be an avoidance of reality.

Years after leaving the Center, I came to understand that emotional responses are like frequencies on a radio dial; if you turn the volume down on one station, you turn it down on all the others at the same time. If you're going to develop joy, laughter, and humor, you will open yourself up to feeling the pain, loss, and sadness of the world, too. Or you can opt, as I had done for most of my life, to turn the volume down and never hear the music at all.

The best way to confront your fears is to stop avoiding the situation you're most afraid of.
—*David D. Burns, M.D.,*
The Feeling Good Handbook

3. *Dare to Be Foolish*

A WOMAN I know told me about the memorable night she received an award at a company banquet. She had just reached the center of the stage when she tripped, dropped the weighty new trophy (which broke) on her host's toe, then ripped her skirt as she bent over to pick up the pieces. "None of this would have been so bad," she added, "except that it was an award for managing the department with the best safety record in the plant."

A colleague of mine still shudders when she recalls the lecture during which, with a perfectly nonchalant flick of the wrist, she sent the water pitcher flying from the podium in a perfect, drenching arc over the front row of the audience.

Another friend, a foreman in a nuclear power plant, told me how once he rushed from home to take charge in a crisis, and of course the television crews were there waiting for him. "After things calmed down," he said, "I went back to my apartment just in time to see myself on the evening news. Was I ever horrified.

Apparently, I'd been in such a hurry to get to the plant that I put my wig on backward—it looked as if a possum had died on top of my head. But, you know, I think the worst thing was that, even though I knew my crew noticed, nobody ever mentioned it to me."

Each of these incidents reflects the old comedic formula: *If it happens to you, it's funny; if it happens to me, it's tragic.*

When we slip on the proverbial banana peel, most of us want to disappear, die, or maybe just machine-gun the witnesses. At one time or another we've all felt some version of:

"If I fail at this, I'm done for."

"I made such a fool of myself, they're going to kill me."

"I was so embarrassed, I could have died."

Clearly, embarrassment is a big deal. We want others to see us as wise, not foolish; graceful, not clumsy; winners, not losers. Above all, we dread having people observe our humiliation—unless, of course, we've been embarrassed as a group. (In recent years, when I came across a survey showing people to be more afraid of public speaking than nuclear war, I instantly understood! After all, following a nuclear war, what's to be embarrassed about if *everyone* left alive is a walking night-light?)

Unfortunately, our perfectly normal fear of foolishness is also the number one barrier to lightening up. We dread that others may think we're absurd—ridiculous, incongruous, or unreasonable; yet increasing our humor quotient requires us to become connoisseurs of absurdity—*especially* our own.

With the help of the humor skills detailed in this

book, you can rob embarrassing situations like these of their power and learn to see them as funny (or at least, neutral)—even when the joke is on you. But, first, just as I had to face up to and understand my own block—alcohol—we all have to recognize and understand the source and structure of that big fear of being seen as foolish.

From the simply ridiculous to the painfully humiliating, moments of foolishness can change our lives forever; shape our personalities; determine the degree of risk or creative effort we will attempt; and dull our capacity for humor, joy, and laughter. For me, one moment did all that and more.

Horror Story

When I was sixteen years old, my high-school English teacher, Mrs. Johannsen, encouraged me to participate in a speaking contest. (It occurs to me, three decades later, that perhaps she just got tired of my goofing off in class). I hated the idea of public speaking, which didn't seem nearly as macho as football. Because I weighed only 100 pounds, however, football was scarcely the perfect choice for me. I needed some points to get a passing grade in the class, and so I agreed.

With my teacher's constant help, I won the school title, then the district, then the county, and was on my way to the area finals. For the first time in my life, I was winning, and I liked it. I liked it *a lot*. Unfortunately, I became more enamored of being a winner than working like one. It had been so easy to demolish the local competition. I became smug. I began to see myself with the national title, a new life, a beautiful girlfriend, a hot-rod Ford, and a college scholarship to Stanford.

Mrs. Johannsen tried to persuade me to keep working on the speech, to polish and practice it daily. I couldn't see it. The competition was some thick-necked football player with a cowlick and a sloping, Neanderthal brow, who dressed like a farm boy in overalls, so why bother?

When we shook hands in the auditorium where we were to present, he said, "I know you're really good. If you win, I hope you go on to the nationals."

I grinned and nodded. That was my plan. First, the area. Then the nationals. Maybe even the internationals! We drew cards; he was to speak first.

At the podium, the boy bumped the microphone, causing feedback to come shrieking out of the speakers. He winced, grinned apologetically, and then proceeded to give one of the most impassioned, intelligent, well-thought-out speeches imaginable. His voice was deep, his tones were superbly modulated, his delivery was flawless, and his sincerity made the structural perfection of his talk seem as though it was coming from the heart.

My stomach was grinding like a cement mixer. I knew, I absolutely knew, there was no need for me to get up there when he finished. I prayed he would spit, or drool, or knock over the podium. Anything! In my sixteen-year-old mind, Stanford vanished, the hot rod crashed, the girl of my fantasies slammed the door in my face. I was, before I even stood and spoke, a failure.

After the judges had given my opponent the first standing ovation in the history of the contest, I made my weak-kneed way to the podium. I was praying again, but now I was also trying to gird—whatever that means—my pubescent loins for battle. My fear was becoming rage. I wouldn't quit. I would speak. I would speak like never before. And that anger born of humiliation carried me toward the front of the hall.

Unfortunately, anger increases adrenalin flow, which, in many cases, has a way of making people stupid. My fear, rage, and subsequent tension combined to twist my tongue, bring unnatural spasms to my arms and face, and, in general, lead me to sound something like Pee Wee Herman with a mouthful of litchi nuts.

I was, how do you say, less than impressive. The applause, when I finished, was horridly polite.

So embarrassed I wanted to die?

You bet.

Instead of trying to find humor in the situation, or at least learning a bitter lesson, my shame gained momentum. I stayed away from school for a week, contemplating whether I ought to jump off a cliff or jump on a train heading out of town. Eventually, my experience affected the course of my life in negative and positive ways.

At the time I knew only one thing: I was *never* going to be humiliated like that again.

Go Ahead—Make My Day

Whether you study anthropology, sociology, or psychology, theories differ, but one thing is clear: people are social animals. We **dread** making fools of ourselves *because* foolishness can lead to ridicule, and ridicule, to loss of status or—in the most terrifying extreme— exile. Remember that, for criminals, a sentence of solitary confinement is second in severity only to death.

Some theorize that the need for community is learned; others believe it's genetic, a survival mechanism woven into our DNA. Clearly, as a species, people were clumsier, slower, and less well armed than a lot of other carnivores. Through a combination of luck, flexibility, intelligence (which was not necessarily greater than that of dolphins), and, most important, **teamwork and cooperation,** they survived and thrived.

Although Hollywood tells us otherwise, if it were possible to pit a muscleman like Arnold Schwarzenegger against a tiger, the tiger would win. But allow a group of people—even total nerds—to hunt, or merely build a housing development in the habitat of the beast, and eventually the human tribe will triumph.

That our craving for acceptance from friends, families, and communities seems engineered into the human species may partially explain the battered woman who calls the police for help in the midst of a domestic crisis, only to fight them off when they try to take her husband away (better the brute she knows than no one at all); or gang members willing to risk death rather than lose status in the group. I've often wondered if actors and public figures are canonized because they say and do absurd things, risking rejection *for us.* (Do we respect their courage, ego, or craziness? Or am I just looking for a way to elevate what I do for a living?)

Anatomy of a Bummer:
The General-Adaptation Syndrome

Foolishness, embarrassment, and failure cause the average human being considerable stress. As many of you are aware, it was the work of endocrinologist Hans Selye, a pioneer in "psychosomatic medicine," which began to illuminate the connection between *perceived stress*—whether physical (a missile has been fired at your city) or psychological (you're unzipped while addressing a group of nuns)—and bodily symptoms. Selye's theory of the *general-adaptation syndrome* divides our reaction to perceived danger into three phases.

Stage 1: The Alarm Reaction

Our universal reaction to perceived danger is the fight-or-flight response. Without it, we probably would not have survived on the planet. (Because, although **teamwork** may have allowed us to best the tiger, at times teamwork meant, "Hey, Og, let's run like hell!")

Within hundredths of a second, the pulse quickens, increasing blood flow and pressure. Adrenalin is pumped into the body to increase strength; lactic acid begins to boil in the muscles to prepare them for effort; the chemical cortisol is released that, among other effects, helps blood coagulate more quickly (just in case Og can't run faster than the tiger). The bowels may loosen and—how can I say this delicately?—help to lighten the load so that you can move on down the road.

The effects of fight or flight enable us to hit harder, jump higher, run faster, and scream louder. It's a great system if you need to defend yourself against a street gang. Not so useful in the modern world where, more often than not, the threat is to self-esteem—getting fired, or discovering that your spouse is having an affair with an aerobics teacher (which really gets your heart pumping).

As a short-term reaction, this response may be useful and doesn't harm our bodies. If the "stressor" persists, however—for instance, you are not only fired, but denied unemployment; or your spouse leaves you for the aerobics teacher—the alarm reaction leads to the next stage of the general-adaptation syndrome.

Stage 2: Resistance

In the second stage, our brain chemistry adjusts and the body appears to develop a tolerance for the stressor much as it would for addictive drugs. At the same time we become less resistant to other stressors. Consider the widower who has adapted well to the stress of living alone, but who, upon receiving bad news from the grandchildren, succumbs quickly to physical illness.

If the stressor is something that won't go away— unrelenting change, a job we hate, or the IRS contracting a persistent interest in us—our heightened arousal may become destructive.

Stage 3: Exhaustion

In the third and final phase of the general-adaptation syndrome, as exposure to the perceived threat continues, our heightened hormonal secretions lead to pathological changes in the organs. "The anterior pituitary and adrenal cortex are unable to continue secreting their hormones at the increased rate, with the result that the organism can no longer adapt to the continuing stress," says William W. Ruch, professor of psychology at the University of Southern California.

"Many of the physiological dysfunctions which originally appeared during the alarm reaction begin to reappear," Ruch adds. As the exhaustion phase continues, the end result can be emotional illness, disease, even death. This stage has been connected with "voodoo death" by various psychologists.

What about the "voodoo job," perhaps, or the "voodoo family"?

The medical discipline of *psychoneuroimmunology*, introduced a bit in Chapter 1, builds on the work of Selye and others, investigating the delicate connections among:

psychology—study of the mind
neurology—study of how the nervous system communicates with the body
immunology—study of how the immune system functions, or fails to function, to keep you alive.

PNI (which is a lot easier to say and spell) is a field of study that was unnamed prior to 1981. The major revelation from this discipline is that prolonged stress may cause not only a direct attack on the organs (see the exhaustion stage above), but also a direct and measurable effect on the immune system.

In her landmark book, *Mending the Mind, Minding the Body*, Joan Borysenko, Ph.D., describes some of the most important research in PNI. One experiment performed on a group of dental students showed the connection between pre-exam stress and their incidence of catching colds. "We discovered," Borysenko writes, "that the stress of examination periods reduced the level of a particular antibody in saliva, an antibody that is part of the first line of defense against colds."

Selye's work and subsequent studies in PNI show that the connection between our thoughts and our health is absolutely real and quite complex. Borysenko says, "Our minds have the ability to spin out endless imaginings that are quite real to the body, imaginings that unleash the hormones and neuropeptides that tell the body what to do."

Because lightening up requires us to overcome our fear of foolishness, some of the exercises described in pages to come might make you uncomfortable. That's quite normal. Luckily, the humor skills that make you feel ridiculous can also help you learn the difference between an attacking tiger and job insecurity. With practice, you can turn terror into excitement, threat into challenge, and straw into gold! (Sorry, I got carried away.)

Why We Aren't Dead Yet

With bad news more common than dirty air or water, you may wonder how any of us has managed to survive the twentieth century. Luckily, *stress-release valves* were built into the human organism by the designer, which is why so many of us trudge admirably through life despite difficult marriages, boring jobs, and the national deficit. Although this list is far from all-inclusive, these are some of the major tools we human beings have to avert exhaustion or death by stress.

Valve 1: Attitude

Attitude, according to Borysenko, influences our health—including our ability to manage stress—as much as does our behavior (such as smoking, exercise, and diet). Recall Selye's notion that stress is not an event, but a reaction based upon our perception of the event. Perceptions can be changed, although events cannot. In other words, we are free to alter our thinking. Whether we choose to or not is up to us.

Valve 2: Physical Release

Physical exercise: Selye was one of the first to prescribe exercise for relieving the physiological effects of stress. (You shouldn't take an axe to a boss you don't like, but you can play racketball, and tape the boss's picture to the ball.)

Valve 3: Mental Discipline

Mental exercise: In the past two decades, Joan Borysenko, Herbert Benson, and many others have begun to provide and popularize vast quantities of scientific data that prove and explain the benefits of the relaxation response—a "side effect" of meditation.

Not big news to any of the major religions who began to recommend meditation centuries ago, but what is new is that science can now explain (and therefore accept) the mechanics of a technique discovered intuitively so long ago.

Alcoholics Anonymous suggested when the "big book" was published in 1939 that recovered alcoholics learn to meditate instead of drinking to ease their fears and resentments. In 1952, Norman Vincent Peale—a respected pastor and the father of "positive thinking"—popularized the connection between meditation and stress relief in his international bestseller, *The Power of Positive Thinking*.

Valve 4: Humor (of Course)

Deep in the human psyche, people know that if they don't lighten up when things get tough, they're going to tighten up and snap. It was no coincidence that during the Great Depression in the 1930s, Hollywood lowered admission prices to films and produced hundreds of lighthearted comedies and musicals because the audience demanded an escape from economic despair.

Until now, the Depression produced the largest explosion of comedy and humor this country had seen. Today, it's not an economic depression that's fueling the demand, but widespread frustration, panic, and confusion brought about by an unrelenting storm of change. It's no coincidence that, reflecting the Depression hit, "Happy Days Are Here Again," one of the biggest hits of the past few years was Bobby McFerrin's "Don't Worry, Be Happy."

Humaerobics—Hope for a Flabby Sense of Humor

In my seminars I offer people exercises to help recharge their sense of humor. Humaerobics, physical and mental exercises that enhance humor skills, do involve some risk. Think of them as a sort of Outward Bound training program for the terminally serious. In Outward Bound you climb mountains, cross rope bridges, and trek through the wilderness. You survive the experience with more self-confidence, decreased fear of challenge, and a greater sense of teamwork that you can take back to the office. With Humaerobics you make silly noises, peculiar gestures, goofy faces, and somehow survive, too. These ridiculous exercises allow you to take physical risks with the way you look and learn to play a bit.

A colleague in *humoroptics* (the science of seeing silliness), is Steve Allen, Jr., son of comedian Steve

Allen, and, in his spare time, a physician practicing medicine on the East Coast. Steve's other occupation is traveling and lecturing on the health benefits of humor, laughter, and play. He helps people understand how to balance their lives through the metaphor of juggling. When you leave Dr. Allen's workshop, you can juggle—not flaming torches and chainsaws, but cheesecloth scarves. He finds that the juggling experience often expands people's perception of their capabilities. It was from Steve that I learned the difference between stupid and silly.

"Stupid," Dr. Allen says, "means ignorant and uneducated. You do stupid things because you don't know any better. Having fun and playing is not stupid—it is silly."

Silly, Allen points out, derives originally from the Old English *(ge)saelig*, which meant completely happy, blessed. *Silly* was a blessing you wished upon those you loved. It meant to be happy, prosperous, and healthy.

If, in the next few pages, you are tempted to say to yourself, "This is stupid!" take note. It is not stupid, it is silly, a blessing, and good for you—Dr. Allen said so.

If you have the courage to do these exercises wholeheartedly, you will experience decreased fear of foolishness and failure and increased lightheartedness. Knowing that you can survive physical silliness makes risk taking easier. Besides, it's fun.

If, like some people, you can't help but associate silliness with rejection, failure, and even death, take it slowly. Some Japanese and Japanese-Americans especially may have trouble with Humaerobics because *enryo* ("behavioral restraint") matters so much in the traditional Japanese family. But I can think of lots of midwestern Lutherans and New England Congregationalists and Southern Baptists who might have the same problem.

If, as a child, you were punished for silliness or play, you may find physical Humaerobics impossible. That's fine. Stick with the later mental exercises or touchstones, at least in the beginning.

Realize that Humaerobics is not a one-size-fits-all program. I want you to slip into this material at a rate you're comfortable with. Remember, your dread of foolishness is normal; in some circumstances it can serve a useful purpose.

The idea here is to gain enough control that your fears won't keep you from taking healthy risks. In later chapters we'll introduce you to other kinds of humor exercises—all of which are designed to put you back in touch with your desire, capacity, and right to feel good. But first to warm you up . . .

The American Bat Face

Remember when some adult said to you: "Don't make that horrible face! It can stick like that, you know"? Well, in modern history there's only one example of a face getting permanently stuck in a ridiculous expression—Andy Rooney—and he got a job anyway.

Some of the most underused muscles are in the face—at least, in the adult's face. Small children may have a facial range habit pattern of twelve to twenty faces they use during the day. Many adults, by age thirty, have only three. (Some upper management people I've worked with have one—a mask of professional cool that they use for everything from, "Of course I'm

glad you work here, Smithers. What makes you think I'm not?" to, "Yes dear, I love you. Why do you ask?")

It takes practice to loosen up facial muscles and regain access to the wide range of emotional responses we are capable of.

One of the children I worked with gave me this expressive exercise. She said it was the silliest face an adult could make: the American Bat Face.

BEGIN: Stand in front of a mirror, find a funloving group of friends or share this exercise with family members, especially little children.

STEP 1: Place your hand on top of your head, with the fingers pointing straight forward.

STEP 2: Reach down with the middle two fingers and touch the tip of your nose—pull the nose up, flaring the nostrils. (Attractive, eh?)

STEP 3: Flap your tongue in and out of your mouth while making a high-pitched squealing noise.

STEP 4: Say to yourself, several times: "This is not stupid, it's silly. It's a blessing."

Low-Impact Humor Exercises

For those of you who survived the Bat Face—or even enjoyed it—here are some additional techniques to try. Before going on, however, I offer a serious bit of advice: Although these exercises are as safe as any others, do not attempt them while operating heavy equipment.

The Snake Eating Its Tail

This exercise evolved from classes I took in the seventies with one of my Tibetan Buddhist friends, a monk named Thon.

Thon told me that if I was ever to understand life, I would have to first discover the "silliness in seriousness." Because I took myself more seriously than anything else, I was to start by finding the silliness in me.

STEP 1: Thon told me to rise from bed each morning and stand naked in front of a full-length mirror.

STEP 2: With my feet spread wide and my hands on my hips, I was to laugh at myself. It didn't have to be real. Rather, I was to make laughing sounds—ha-ha-ha-ha, ho-ho-ho-ho-, and so on—even if I was in a rotten mood.

STEP 3: I was to do this until the morning when I began the exercise and found myself laughing from the heart.

It sounded stupid (I didn't know yet that it was just silly), but this happened in the seventies, a decade when *stupid* didn't deter me from much. I continued to do the exercise for weeks until, one morning—I still don't know why—my reflection in the mirror struck me as genuinely funny. I noticed how sour I looked. My forehead knotted furiously when I laughed my phony laugh. At that moment I looked myself in the eye and *knew* that I was God's punch line. I lost it.

I tried to stop laughing, but could not. My knees buckled and my chest and stomach ached. The more I looked at myself, the harder I laughed. I ended up on the floor, gasping for breath, and abruptly began crying. Sorrow filled my heart as I began to remember many painful incidents in my life. I was crying as hard as I'd been laughing only a few moments before. Then I saw myself in the mirror again, and even my teary, puffy eyes and miserable expression looked silly. I was crying about things that weren't happening any more. And I started to laugh again!

Finally, I giggled and gasped my way to the bathroom. I decided to take a bath rather than a shower because I was afraid the drain would look funny. What if I laughed, slipped, and cracked my head? I might die laughing! Then, the bathtub looked funny, too, and so I decided to just wash my face. It was a wonderful morning—although I smelled pretty ripe the rest of the day.

My teacher explained to me that I had experienced the Snake Eating Its Tail; I had laughed until I cried, cried until I laughed.

Since those days I've learned that the limbic system, which governs and manages the chemistry of our emotions, is delicately wired; any extreme emotional reaction may trigger its opposite. That's why some people laugh at funerals. Limbic sensitivity causes some people who attend a humor workshop—and laugh more than they have in years—to go home feeling a bit down, or even sad. Feeling is feeling, and when you cut yourself off from feeling bad by suppressing or ignoring your pain, you can also cut yourself off from feeling good.

Now, I consider the Snake Eating Its Tail to be a pretty rigorous humor exercise, although you're welcome to try it.

Stand, Breathe, and Smile

As I began presenting humor workshops, I found that most people were reluctant to strip naked and laugh at themselves in mirrors—except of course for those in advertising. And so I created a modified version of the Snake Eating Its Tail called the Stand, Breathe, and Smile, or SBS.

The exercise is relaxing and silly, and the act of smiling sends a message to your brain—hey, something must be funny around here. As with most humor exercises, the SBS is most effective in a group, even a small group of three or four. Many families practice the exercise together with fun results.

BEGIN: Assume a comfortable sitting position (hint: a chair works).

STEP 1: Count to three, and then . . .

STEP 2: Stand up, taking a deep breath as you rise to your feet.

STEP 3: Smile the biggest grin you can make. Let those teeth show.

STEP 4: Repeat steps 1 through 3 until you:
  A. Start laughing
  B. Get bored
  C. Embarrass yourself
  D. Find you are too tired to get up again
  E. Are done

I often start my humor workshops with the SBS exercise, and it never fails to have a positive effect. Of course, when several hundred people are doing the exercise together, the results are amplified. Laughter *really is* contagious. According to Koestler, "Laughter is a phenomenon of the trigger-releaser type where a sudden turn of the tap may release vast amounts of stored emotions, derived from various, often unconscious sources. . . . "

I know from my experiences with thousands of clients over the years that the SBS has few if any negative side effects. Start your Humaerobics workout with an SBS in the morning as you get out of bed (try a half dozen repetitions if you find you're really enjoying yourself); or, wait until you've had your coffee, tea, or wheat-grass juice, then try it at the breakfast table.

The exercise itself won't change your life, save the rain forest, or keep a perm from going flat. But it might help you stay in touch with your ability to express feeling good in case the opportunity offers itself. After all, if you aren't enjoying your time on the planet, you probably won't do anything about those more cosmic problems anyway.

Photo Funnies

Photo Funnies are truly silly. (Remember silly?) Silly as this exercise sounds, our clients over the years have rated it a terrific tool for reshaping our fears of foolishness into plain fun.

BEGIN: Find one of those photo booths where, for seventy-five cents or a dollar, you can sit down, pull a curtain, and take a four-picture photo strip of yourself. (Hint: If you close the curtain, nobody can see anything but your feet. If your feet have the power to embarrass you, don't let them do anything silly.)

STEP 1: Get four snapshots of yourself looking utterly ridiculous! You don't have to show these to anyone, so let out all the stops: fingers in the nose, ears, and mouth (not necessarily in that order); eyes wide, crossed, squinting; mouth open, tight-lipped, fish-lipped. Go for it. It's good to include a Bat Face.

STEP 2: Grab the photos when the machine spits them out, and carry them in your pocketbook or wallet.

STEP 3: The next time you have to deal with a friend, family member, coworker, employee, or boss— whom you don't quite hate, but wish had been born in Siberia and stayed there—take out those pictures. Study them.

STEP 4: Think. You are not just the problem you are having; you're this too. (Imagine what the other person's photos would look like if they'd had the nerve to do this exercise.)

Use the photos as a tool to regain your sense of humor. Look at them next time you have one of those Christian and Lions meetings with family, staff, or clients (and you're not the lion). What are you worried about? Sneak a peek at your photos, Bubba. You've already made a fool of yourself, and it didn't kill you.

Some people who are nervous about public speaking like to place the photos on the podium so that they can access a humor perspective by glancing at them. (No matter what happens, you won't look this ridiculous again.) At critical moments, Photo Funnies can remind you that you're not just your problems; you're what's in those pictures, too.

If all this seems odd, believe me when I say that it seemed odd to me as well. But why don't you try it for several weeks before making up your mind? Just refrain from making Bat Faces while the nice police officer is writing out your traffic ticket. I tried it once in New Jersey, and the man was not amused.

Now that you have a starting point for exercising your physical sense of play, fun, and humor, please don't overdo it. Pick one exercise of the several offered in this and subsequent chapters, and do it for six weeks. Then add another. Like any exercise program that is to have lasting effects, Humaerobics and humor skills should be built up gradually. It doesn't make much sense to stress yourself out in a rush to lighten up.

Please, Mr. Custer, I Don't Wanna Go . . .

It's normal here for many people to pose these rhetorical questions: "Is this jerk serious? Does he expect me to *do* these things?"

The answer is yes. This jerk hopes you will at least try. Until I began to challenge my fear of foolishness, failure, and embarrassment with Humaerobics, the notion of exercising my physical capacity for humor seemed absurd. (Maybe it is. But that is, after all, what humor is about.)

If you're reading this book at home, how about trying an SBS or Bat Face now? Right now. If you're uneasy, what's scaring you? (I understand your desire to wait if you're in a public library, in a bus, or in some other social situation. But alone? Who are you afraid might see you? You?)

It *is* easier to do these exercises in a group where hundreds or thousands of others are joining you; at least then it's a community commitment. Going for a Silly Solo your first time out takes courage. Why should you try? Well, taking these first, silly steps is a way of letting yourself know that you care enough about yourself to learn how to lighten up. Or, as the great actress Ethel Barrymore put it: "You grow up the day you have your first good laugh—at yourself."

THE
FIRST
HUMOR
SKILL

Few would deny that the capactiy for humor, like hope, is one of humanity's most potent antidotes for the woes of Pandora's box.

> —George Vaillant,
> **Adaptation to Life**

4. Escape from the Center of the Universe

DO you remember the "Sartre-sky and Hutch" skit on *Saturday Night Live*? . . . the story of of a street-smart young cop and a French existentialist philosopher. They had the "Hutch" character in his leather jacket, and then Dan Ackroyd running around with a pipe and beret muttering "C'est l'absurd!" about every twenty seconds.

The first humor skill that I came to understand was a disciplined **humor perspective** that allowed me to access absurdity, even in the most difficult situations. **Absurdity** typically means "ridiculously incongruous" and "unreasonable," that is, a happy existentialist, a well-behaved two-year-old, the Easter Possum, simplified tax forms, any weather report, canvas underwear, the thrill of defeat.

When we counter adversity with a humor perspective, we become equal to or rise above our problems. For people coming out of a rough spot in their lives, recognizing the absurdities of prior behavior is essential for regaining that all-important sense of joy in being alive.

A friend of mine who is a recovering alcoholic said it neatly: "Today I'm sober; I can make choices. When the car gets dirty, I take it to a car wash. When I was drinking, I'd get so depressed about having to drive a dirty car, I'd go out and buy a fifth of scotch—which cost more than the car wash."

A healthy sense of the absurd was at the core of the Center for Attitudinal Healing's approach to dealing with life's most difficult moments. I remember a boy named Bennie at the Center who was about to undergo surgery. As his parents approached his hospital room, they had themselves worked up for a painful conversation, but as they neared the open door they were startled by the sound of children's laughter. Inside, Jerry Jampolsky and several of their son's friends from the Center stood around the boy's bed. Bennie was wearing a girl's wig and laughing so hard, he had tears in his eyes.

Jerry explained that the kids had been talking openly about the operation. One of the children had asked Benny to confess his greatest fear. Was it the idea that he might never wake up, or the pain of recovery?

"It's none of that stuff," Bennie said. "It's that I might die and have to go see God when I'm bald like this."

Every child in the room instantly understood. After losing his hair to radiation treatments, Bennie—like most of the kids at the Center—had been teased by schoolmates.

"That's not a problem," one little girl had said. "You can borrow mine." With a broad grin and a flourish,

she took off her long red wig and offered it to her bedridden buddy.

With the wig on, Bennie studied his reflection in
the mirror. Seconds later, he started laughing. Soon,
Jerry and the other kids joined in. Each of them
tried the wig, then gave it back to Bennie. Nobody told
him he shouldn't feel that way, nobody made fun of
his fear, nobody shamed him. His friends helped him
find the absurdity in his fears so that he could con-
quer them.

TO learn this first humor skill—accepting absurdity—you need not become an alcoholic, develop cancer, or attempt to crash-land a ruptured DC-10. You
do, however, have to make sure that you understand
your place in the universal scheme.

The Known Universe

Center

You are here

The Known Universe

Notice that the Center of the Universe is approxi-
mately in the middle. Notice, too, that your position
is light years away from the center. Be calm. We'd all
like to be in charge of the universe, or at least control
a majority of the stock. A desire for control is nor-

mal (more on control in Chapter 5). Probably, nobody reading this book got up this morning, looked in the mirror, and said: "Hello, Center of the Universe, how are you doing, you gorgeous life form, you? Let's go kick 'em around a little." But when you find yourself ignoring everyone's needs but your own, that's when you're heading for that big galactic bullseye.

Obviously this confrontation presents problems for you as a social being, but the real whammy comes when "your" world—the one you think you control—moves in a direction you didn't plan on, don't approve of, and have no intention of participating in. Then you've got an even bigger problem.

The Center of the Universe is a killing position I tried to hold down for much of my life. Every glitch was mine to fix, and I loved taking the credit when things worked well. But when disaster struck, that was my fault too.

Certainly, we need to take responsibility for our actions during periods of crisis and change. The degree of responsibility, however, is a matter of balancing our reactions. Even when Captain Haynes was riding that DC-10 toward Sioux City, he managed to keep his perspective—the awareness that he was part of a team. When Denny Fitch, the off-duty United flight instructor, entered the cockpit and knelt to help with the throttles, the exchange went like this.

Fitch: Hi, Al. Denny Fitch.
Haynes: How do you do, Denny.
Fitch: I'll tell you what. We'll have a beer when this is all done.
Haynes: Well, I don't drink, but I'll sure as . . . have one.

What would a captain *at the Center of the Universe* have done, sitting there at the controls of his faltering jetliner, when some guy walks in from the passenger compartment to offer a little helpful advice? I think we can imagine some colorful language, and then maybe Denny Fitch bouncing back to his seat on his head.

MY grandmother used to say, "Everybody wants to be the director of the universe. The trouble is, the job's already taken!"

Whether or not you agree with Gramma, I've learned from experience that I don't want the job. Three warning signals indicate that I've lost the capacity to sense absurdity in myself and my problems. Instead of working to control my perspective, I've assumed responsibility for the cosmos—again.

Top-Three Warning Signs: Are You the Center of the Universe?

Number 3: *Nothing* is *ever* your *fault*

Blaming others when things go wrong gives us the illusion of control. We identified the source of the problem and, just as we thought, somebody else screwed things up! Faultfinding provides a short-lived victory. If it is *their* fault, we have to wait for *them* to change. Just how successful have you been, lately, in changing other people? How successful would Captain Haynes have been if he had devoted his time to figuring out whose damned fault it was that the engine had blown? Is it true that questions always come in threes? Or is it fours?

Number 2: *Everything* is *always* your *fault*

Back in the sixties, I was befriended by a young woman who truly believed she controlled the universe. When she was around, we were innocent. When it was raining, Fly Fire would say something like, "Wow, I got so bummed out last night, the world started to cry for me." Of course, when the sun came out it was because Fly was in a good mood.

We all know a Fly Fire—unless we're busy being one. This condition usually happens for me when a seminar I'm about to present becomes the most important event since the first Apollo moon flight.

I begin to assume responsibility for everything. I become certain that the entire planet ought to operate in support of my magnificent goals, and when it refuses to go along with the deal I get tired, irritable and stressed-out. I become convinced that if I'd only worked a little harder, done a little more . . . or better yet if *you* had, or . . . or, something, then it all would have been absolutely perfect.

Number 1

Any combination of 2 and 3 above.

Escape from the Center

You can hope that some dramatic, painful, or life-threatening experience will grant you a humor perspective, but most people prefer a less random approach. Learning to appreciate the absurdity in adversity *can be* simple—not easy, just simple. Over the years, research, participant input, and blind luck have

led me to a package of tools that I hope will be of value
to you.

A Humor Library

Clearly, I needed daily help in remembering that the
world, with all its injustice, depravity, and bad-
tempered film reviewers, really did have an absurdly
humorous edge. Being open to the absurdity in my
deepest convictions helps keep them from mutating
into prejudices or obsessions. To remind myself, I began to collect **cartoons** lampooning serious subjects—
especially subjects dear to my heart. What started out
several years ago as a shelf or two of materials has become my Absurdity Annex. I found and collected examples of a humor perspective everywhere: **books,
magazines, newspapers, letters from friends**, humorous **postcards, posters,** and **biographies** of people who
had known how to access absurdity in adversity.

Whenever someone reminds me to practice what I
preach, the annex is usually my first stop. Lately, I've
added **video** and **audio** tapes as well.

One family who attended my seminar makes it a
practice now to tape record stories about the things
they "can now look back on and laugh about, but were
embarrassed by at the time." They add those tapes to
their own humor library, which they intend to pass on
to their children and grandchildren.

I've just started asking my friends to put their favorite absurdity anecdotes on audio or video tape and
send them to me. (Considering the kind of friends I
have, I may have to build an addition on to the house.)

My humor library offers a wealth of proof—to my
mind at least—that without humor skills, there is no

ultimate triumph over tragedy, no joy in the journey, no sense in the nonsense of it all.

A Humor Inventory (HI)

My friends in "Twelve Step" and many other treatment programs use a written inventory as part of their recovery. The idea is to write down the resentment, anger, and fear that weakened them until addictive behavior masked those feelings. I was so impressed with how effective the inventory was that I began experimenting with a written Humor Inventory (HI).

The inventory is often the turning point in helping people to regain health, self-respect, and a humor perspective. Of course it is possible to overcome any addiction and remain sick, full of self-loathing, and completely humorless, but I don't think a book on that subject is necessary.

My own HI helped me to remember, recognize, and rearrange reactions that had warped my humor perspective for decades. That first stumbling attempt has evolved into a tool that many clients think is their most effective device for regaining a healthy point of view. (This approach is especially helpful if you are more analytical than physical in your approach to the world, or if you are so shy that Humaerobics are unbearably difficult. For people who are physically limited—bedridden or in a wheelchair—the humor inventory can be invaluable.)

A written HI allows us to take stock of positive and negative influences upon our humor perspective. Most important, it allows us to choose which experiences we want to cherish, and which we want to forgive and forget. The HI itself is simple. It focuses on the times in our lives when most of us make decisions about humor, joy, lightheartedness, and fun. The idea is to explore the most prominent experiences by writing down:

A. What happened . . .
B. How it made you feel . . .
C. What were you left with?
D. What can you do about it?

A Serious Scenario

If you find yourself unable to access the information, exercises, and suggestions in this book—especially a Humor Inventory—put it aside. Childhood is often painful, and some experiences can cripple our emotional health and our capacity for humor. The latest statistics indicate that as many as 40 percent of us were physically or sexually abused as children at least once by someone we trusted. Such experiences legitimately create fear and withdrawal—often without our conscious memory of the event that caused our reaction in the first place. We may equate any extreme emotional expression with trouble, pain, or threat.

If you are truly blocked, consider getting a therapist's help. Please. You can always come back to the HI later.

Onward and Inward

My first HI included a traumatic incident that distorted my humor sense for years. I'll use it here as an example.

Step 1: What Happened?

When I was ten years old I entered puberty like a truck through a plate-glass window. My voice dropped, as did parts of my anatomy, and I sprouted a thick covering of body hair. I looked like a scrawny, underfed otter. When we had to undress for gym, my male classmates would laugh, bark, and call me "dog-boy."

Step 2: How Did It Make Me Feel?

It made me feel isolated, cast out, and creepy looking.

Step 3: What Was I Left With?

I was left with the idea that humor always injured someone. I learned to think of jokes as weapons, and teasing as punishment. As a result, I too used teasing against other people. I hated people who teased me.

Step 4: What Can I Do About It?

I want to stop using humor as a weapon, and respond to those who tease me with something other than hatred.

The Stages of Humor (or, the First Stage out of Town)

The following pages provide you with a chronological approach to the HI method. The headings are suggestions, not rules. Don't be limited by them. I have included questions and blank space here, instead of in an appendix, so that you can fill in your responses before you get distracted by work, what's left of the economy, or global warming.

Stage 1: Grade School—Ages Five to Eleven

When humor is confused with aggression, teasing is the usual result. If you were teased about your gender, name, race, religion, weight, planet of birth, and so on, you may want to pay particular attention to those experiences in your inventory. Having been a teasing victim often leaves us with a sense of anger, self-doubt, or fear of embarrassment that can distort our adult humor perspective.

1. Was I teased as a child? Describe what happened:

2. How did it make me feel? Angry? Fearful? Describe:

3. What was I left with? What did I conclude? Do I still equate humor with teasing?

4. What can I do about it?

Perhaps, reversing the victim role, you used teasing as a way of getting attention, or of striking out at others. That behavior may carry over and narrow your present humor perspective to one of combat and sarcasm.

Sarcasm, by the way, comes from the Greek *sarkazo,* which means to tear at flesh like a dog. That may be why, when I get bitter and sarcastic with my staff, they let me know it by leaving a dog biscuit on my desk. (Milk Bones don't really taste that bad, especially when you're in a rotten mood.)

1. As a child, did I tease others? Describe what happened:

2. How did it make me feel?

3. What was I left with? What did I conclude? Am I still doing it?

4. What can I do about it?

As with all the inventory headings, you may be lucky enough to remember positive humor experiences. Be sure to include them. One of mine was a joke my grandmother played on me when I was about seven years old. The funny part was that I didn't get it until years later.

When I asked her how she could always tell when I was lying, she said, "Well, when people lie, it makes them smell bad."

I was amazed. Could it really be so simple? I was twelve years old when I realized that some very honest people had B.O. Gramma's story, however, did accomplish her main goal. As a kid, I hated to bathe, but after she let me in on the secret connection between lies and lather, I showered daily.

1. What positive associations with humor do I recall from my childhood? Describe what happened:

2. How did these events make me feel?

3. What was I left with? What did I conclude? Am I still doing it?

4. Keep or change?

Stage 2: Junior High—Ages Twelve to Fifteen

Audience members often say that they are still living with a fear of foolishness and failure that formed during their early teens. At that time kids want acceptance. The fear of foolishness and failure is a dominant force in life. If you've ever spent time listening to thirteen-year-olds, you know they are embarrassed by just about anything, especially their parents: "Parents? I don't have parents. I live in a box in an alley. Got no parental units at all."

In our teen years we are easily embarrassed because we are at the edge of our world, so to speak. Nothing lies beyond *this* because *this* is as far as we've been. Nobody else's experience seems relevant. A humiliating dating disaster, an "embarrassing" parent, that moment of public failure, really *is* the worst thing that's ever happened to us. Often, some well-meaning adult makes things worse by saying: "Hey, it's no big deal; that's nothing. Come on, snap out of it. Don't be such a crybaby."

After all, the message seems to be, if you were being grown-up about this, if you weren't such a weakling, you'd understand. Teens often learn in such situations that "adults don't feel." Now, in addition to feeling foolish, they feel guilty (which seems really foolish).

Try to recall if your feelings were encouraged or discouraged as a teenager. What kind of humor role models did you have? Can you remember an episode during those years that was especially embarrassing? Does that moment still affect your behavior?

1. What embarrassing moments do I recall from my early teen years? Describe what happened:

2. How did these events make me feel?

3. What was I left with? What did I conclude? Am I still basing my life on outmoded decisions?

4. What can I do about it?

Stage 3: High School—Ages Fifteen to Eighteen

Many people experience a hardening of humor attitudes in high school. After all, it is a time of maddening mixed messages. At one moment parents are telling us to "Grow up and act like an adult!" At the next they're insisting, "You're not old enough for that yet." At the same time nature is reducing us to pulsing, throbbing, aching heaps of humorless hormones. The result is often the onset of "terminal cool," a state of being that includes passive aggression: learning how to irritate our elders by doing nothing at all. Our humor perspective often suffers.

1. What embarrassing moments do I recall from my high school years? Describe what happened:

2. How did these events make me feel?

3. What was I left with? What did I conclude? Am I still basing my life on outmoded decisions?

4. What can I do about it?

Stage 4: College and Career—Ages Eighteen to Twenty-nine

If we choose to go to college we are up against more social and academic potential for failure. Many of us learn to take fewer and fewer risks along the way. Achievement as an end in itself begins to dull any joy in learning that may have survived childhood. Some people begin to avoid classes that don't directly translate into dollars, and a habit is set for life: If there's nothing in it but fun, it's not worth the effort.

The other response might be that we indulge only in what is fun, and ignore or give minimal attention to the work that needs to be done. As a result we may feel that we've "blown it" and try to compensate later in life by overworking. Can you recall any experiences that helped shape your understanding of a balance between silliness and seriousness?

Launching into a career (or, a more likely event in today's world, a series of careers), we learn that our job is to "kill" the competition—or be "killed." Foolishness means we're airheads. Laughter means we're "not taking our work seriously enough." Embarrassment means that young punk who does a better job than we do. Failure means job loss. We either tighten up and break down or burst into flurries of anger-driven activity, none of which helps develop a positive humor perspective. What events, people, or experiences have affected your understanding of the relation between work and play?

1. What embarrassing moments in my adult education affected me most? Describe what happened:

2. How did these events make me feel?

3. What was I left with? What did I conclude? Am I still basing my life on those decisions?

4. What can I do about it?

Stage 5: Parenthood—Whenever

If you managed to escape having your humor perspective twisted until now, your first child can change all that. There you are with your significant other ("other than what?" I always wonder) and poof, you're not the only ego in the home that needs feeding.

Now, you're guru, guide, and guardian of a completely helpless infant. As your social life changes (that is, disappears) and your priorities shift from Ferrari to formula, your sense of humor can get dimmer than the night-light by the crib. This is a critical time to access absurdity in adversity. It is, in fact, a perfect time to retrain yourself in silliness.

At about six to eight weeks, the baby begins smiling. (No, Gramma, it's not just gas.) In fact, babies will smile at almost any silly face you make; every goonie sound you can concoct is likely to elicit that wonderful, chubby-cheeked, all-encompassing blessing of baby's gummy grin.

Try a Bat Face, or do your Humaerobics with the baby. Somewhere before the twelfth week, the kid will laugh. (That's the sound you sometimes hear other than crying and screaming.) If you can take a deep breath and consider the infant a teacher, you can learn all sorts of wonderful new faces to use in your Photo Funnies.

In this inventory, pay attention to how that first child may have affected your sense of humor. If you haven't yet experienced parenting, consider preparing for it with a lot of laughs—you'll need them. If you don't have children of your own, you have a wonderful alternative—other people's kids! It's great, really. You can play with them, get them laughing, giggling, making faces and, in general, going utterly stark raving looney—then you can leave! (This is a method experienced parents call "Grandparent's Revenge.")

Finally, try to avoid the classic antiabsurdity attitudes that are passed on from one generation to the next. I'm sure most of you have heard them or are sharing them with your own kids.

- "Grow up, get serious!" (Growing up is getting serious? Is that all?)
- "Wipe that stupid smile off your face!" (Smiling is stupid? No. It's silly.)
- "Act your age!" (Usually uttered by a parent to a three-year-old who is, indeed, acting his or her age. The parent really means, "Act my age! I can't handle three!")

1. What were—or do I hope will be—my first experiences with parenting and humor? Describe:

2. How did these events make me feel?

3. What was I left with? What did I conclude?

4. What can I do about it?

Stage 6: Middle Years—Ages Thirty to Sixty-five (That Is, If You Believe the Government)

Too busy, too busy, too busy. These are our "productive years" and most of us find we're too busy to worry about play, laughter, and humor. We're obsessed by time. "What happened to the time? Where did the time go? I'm out of time! I don't have the time to relax or fool around right now. Later. Later. Maybe this weekend, maybe on my vacation, maybe when I retire, maybe when I die, I don't know."

Humor skills, like your checkbook, need occasional infusions to help maintain balance. No deposits in your checking account, and you're out of funds. No investment in humor, and you're out of sorts.

A phrase that helps me maintain a healthy "humor balance" was given to me by Eleanor, a young hospice volunteer who was never too busy to help her clients. "You can always spend more money," she said, "but there's only so much time to be spent living."

1. What is, will be, or has been my experience with humor in relation to my "middle years"?

2. What are the feelings that evolve(d) out of these events?

3. What was I left with? What did I conclude?

4. What can I do about it?

Stage 7: Elder Years—About Four Years Older Than I'll Ever Be

The elders in our lives offer us either hope or hopelessness; it depends on where we look. Many people more than sixty or seventy years old seem too tired or too lonely to enjoy themselves. But actor, entrepreneur and athlete Paul Newman is a professional race-car driver in his mid-sixties (and I'm entirely too sophisticated to make a pun about his ability to race hearts as well).

The most humorous and mentally energetic person I've met to date was 101-year-old Sylvie Washington.

"I love to dance," Sylvie told me one day. Then, she stopped and shuffled her feet, wiggled her hands slightly, and said. "Oh, I know it don't look like much on the outside, C.W., but, inside, I'm tearin' the place apart!"

Perhaps you've been fortunate enough to know an elder who made getting older seem like an adventure rather than a terror. Unfortunately, in Western culture many—if not most—images of elders are negative. As a society we are still guilty of shunting the elderly into special "homes" away from the interaction that keeps them, and us, sensitive to the cycle of love, laughter, and loss. True, some elders have chosen to isolate themselves in retirement communities, but I suspect many of them do so rather than face the ageist attitudes in our culture.

If you don't consider yourself an elder, you can still include that time and space in your inventory. Just envision what you want your status as an elder to be. Do you see a joyful person? One who constructed a humor perspective and aged without growing old? What is the most positive image you can create for yourself?

1. What absurdities and humor do I (will I) see in being older? Describe:

2. How do I feel about aging?

3. What do I want to be like?

4. What can I do about it?

Stage 8: Miscellaneous Incidents That Seem Pertinent to Your Humor Perspective

1. What else shaped my humor perspective? Describe:

2. How did these events make me feel?

3. What was I left with? What did I conclude?

4. What can I do about it?

That's it. Almost.

The Final Step: A Telling Experience

(Okay, I didn't mention this before, but that's because I didn't want to scare you.) The final step with an HI is to read the entire thing to someone. Don't panic. You don't have to—in fact you shouldn't—stop a stranger on the street and ask her to listen to your humor inventory. But the best way to be free of distorted attitudes, as well as to clarify your strengths, is to expose them to the light. I hope you know someone who can be trusted—a friend, family member, rabbi, minister, priest, therapist, or witch doctor—who doesn't demand that you be either heroic or logical all the time. The idea here is *not* to look for deeply buried memories, but simply to get a clearer picture of your humor history, so that you can make conscious choices about your humor perspective.

One client, whose HI particularly embarrassed him, wasn't willing to read it to anyone. He told me later that he'd wanted to forget it, but just hanging on to his discoveries made him feel "really stuffed up and stuck." His solution was unusual but effective. He sat down with his three-month-old infant daughter, Jessie, and read it to her in French.

Not knowing what her dad was doing, but finding it alternately worth giggling or gurgling over, the child listened for nearly an hour until her pop was done.

"It was silly," the man told me. "There were times when I remembered things that made me cry, and Jessie would start giggling or spit up, and it seemed like such a perfect commentary that I'd start laughing. Afterward I felt lighter than I had in years. I realized that what I'd discovered about myself wasn't all that awful. A few weeks later, I was able to share the inventory with my wife, in English."

He went on to explain that his wife was so intrigued, she did an inventory of her own and read it to both Jessie and to him. "Jessie spit up for my wife, too, which amused her as much as it had amused me. I'm convinced that the experience has helped all of us lighten up and find more fun and foolishness in our family."

Now, find that trusted life form and read it to him, her, or it.

More Humaerobics?

Yep. The physical exercises detailed in the last chapter are wonderful support tools for developing a humor perspective as well. After a lifetime of doubt, concern, worry, loss, pain, change, and frustration, paying some attention to the pursuit of play, humor, and laughter doesn't mean you're a terrible, frivolous person. It means that you care enough about yourself, your family, your friends, and your work to make sure that you're as strong, resilient, and effective as possible. Try adding the following exercise to the Stand, Breathe, and Smile and the American Bat Face as part of a quick morning workout.

Exercise 1: The Shake 'n' Face

This exercise is based on our infant learning experiences of laughter, smiling, and play.

BEGIN: To do it, you simply place both feet on the floor (as opposed to the ceiling?), let the hands hang by your sides (pray tell, where else would they hang?) and, slowly at first, then more rapidly, repeat this sequence of body and facial movements with the accompanying sounds.

STEP 1: Shaking the right arm, vigorously but not violently, you grin widely, exposing the teeth, and emit a loud "eeeeee" noise at the same time. (Yes, try it.)

STEP 2: Shaking the left arm, open the mouth wide in the Dental Position, and make a loud "ahhhhhh" sound. (Don't wimp out—give it some energy.)

STEP 3: Now, being careful, use a chair or a friend to steady yourself, and gently shake the right leg while emitting a long groan through "bubble lips"—you know, bubble lips? Like a baby blowing bubbles. (Refer to an infant if memory fails you.)

STEP 4: The sequence is completed with a shaking of the left leg while making any noise you can as your tongue flaps in and out of your mouth.

Got it? Good. Go ahead, try it. (Unless you're reading this passage in a bookstore, and intend to return here some day.) Obviously, you might want to practice all your Humaerobics, at first, in the privacy of an underground bunker. On the other hand, if you'd prefer that the neighbors never come over to borrow anything . . .

(Remember, these are just suggestions.)

REVIEW:
So far, we've covered:
A. My miserable life.
B. Your miserable life.
C. A Humor Door for gaining a fresh perspective.

Humor is a means of obtaining pleasure in spite of the distressing affects that interfere with it.

> —*Sigmund Freud,* Jokes and Their
> Relation to the Unconscious

5. Take Yourself Lightly and Your Work or Problem Seriously

Pigs, Pride, and Perspective

Gather a passel of piglets in a muddy corral, then add a dozen farm kids dressed in their raggediest clothes. Turn the panicked pigs loose to run amok and send the kids in to slip and slide after them. Shrieking in glee, each child attempts to be the first to capture and pull a porker across the finish line. Surround this scene of pandemonium with grandstands full of parents, grandparents, and less-courageous peers who cheer on the participants, and you have a glorious bit of Americana that demonstrates, among other things, how desperate for entertainment we all were before MTV.

I was six years old when I participated in my first, and only, 4-H Greased Pig Grab. I came in last. Thirteen pigs, twelve kids—and everyone else caught at least one.

That woeful day, I trudged into the bleachers where my grandmother sat watching the event. After a few moments she looked me in the eyes and said, "Butchie, you did real well."

"What do you mean?" I asked.

She patted me on the head.

"Way I see it," Gramma said, "you got it half right that time."

"But, I didn't even catch a pig," I moaned.

"You were right to take chasin' the pig seriously— it's about as important as most things people chase after. But you shouldn't take your *self* so serious."

"Oh," I said, although I had no idea what she was getting at. I supposed a pig derby *was* kind of lame compared to other mud-based pursuits some people take all too seriously. But the experience did leave me with a perverse sense of joy in knowing that those footballs are made of pigskin. The little suckers deserve it, as far as I'm concerned.

A Walk on the Weird Side

About thirty years later, a fourteen-year-old cancer patient named Teddy taught me the lesson that Gramma had been trying to get across.

Teddy was, in his own words, "pretty weird," meaning that he liked acting silly. When a nurse new to administering his chemotherapy asked how he was feeling, Teddy frequently barked like a dog, clucked like a chicken, or hissed like a snake.

Most of the nurses went along with him, and his treatments became marked by lighthearted exchanges of animal sounds. Teddy never ignored his pain or tried to cover it up: when he hurt, he hurt, and he let

you know. But in the midst of excruciating discom-
fort, he was one of the most playful, relaxed kids I had
ever been around.

I once heard Teddy sum it up in this way: "I'm Teddy
and I have cancer. I'm not cancer with Teddy attached," he told a group of kids at a hospice gathering. "Most parts of you are healthy. I think when you
forget to take care of the healthy part, and just keep
working on the sick part, more of you starts to get
sick faster."

One of the new clients, a girl of about twelve, asked
him, "So, if I ignore the sick part, it might get sad and
go away?"

"I don't think so, because you still have to keep trying to make the sick part well. It won't help if you
just pretend it isn't there." He paused a moment.
"Look, sometimes I'm sick, sometimes I vomit—like
after the chemo. Sometimes I hurt a lot. But it isn't
always that way. We have cancer. Cancer doesn't have
us."

Taking ourselves lightly and our problems seriously
requires *discipline.* For Teddy, that discipline meant
affirming where the disease stopped and where he, the
person, began.

When the Going Gets Tough . . .

According to conventional wisdom, if you want to
overcome your problem you have to kick it in, bear
down, gear up, pedal to the metal, shoulder to the
wheel, nose to the grindstone, and remember . . . no
pain, no gain. *When the going gets tough, the tough
get going.* (A 1991 survey from Louis Harris and Associates for *Prevention* magazine said that "two-thirds

of adults regularly experience stress in their lives, but most are doing something about it." The survey also stated that 64 percent of adults are overweight. I can't help wondering if, when the going gets tough, the tough aren't going to the refrigerator.)

But why do we choose to take everything so seriously that we often beat ourselves up? Simple, really.

1. It's instinctive.
2. We want control.

A few years ago I attended a lecture by John Cleese, of Monty Python fame, and an adamant champion of humor in business. He was asked if he thought there were times when humor could not help a person.

He replied that of course there were such times. "If you're attacking a machine gun emplacement, it's no time for jokes, pies in the face, or dropping your trousers to amuse the enemy; it's time to get tough and get the job done," he said. "But when the job is done, you had better find something to laugh about, or spend some time relaxing and having fun. Otherwise, you'll be attacking that machine gun emplacement for the rest of your life."

We are far more likely to be stressed-out by "tough" issues involving family, environmental, social, political, personal, and professional threats than by physical danger. In cases of chronic stress, tightening up and slamming through—throwing more time, money, muscle, and energy at the problem—can quickly wear us down. It's like trying to cure a brain tumor by beating the patient's head against a wall.

The responses that helped us survive centuries of physical danger are rarely effective in combating chronic stress. S. J. Lachman pointed out in the early sixties that when "emotional activity or reactivity is sufficiently frequent or prolonged or intense, [like, perhaps, reading this sentence] it becomes maladaptive or destructive, leading to physiological aberration or structural damage to the organism, and even to death." He concluded, "Thus, an organism may be injured or destroyed by its own defenses." In other words, the mechanisms designed to protect us from stress can kill us.

"I'm an Excellent Driver"

We live in fear of "losing control." We speak of controlling forest fires, teenagers, tempers, thoughts, actions, feelings, and destinies. When we're "out of control" we feel powerless, overwhelmed, and helpless. From helplessness we regress to fear, paranoia, and paralysis, or we explode in desperate acts of violence against ourselves and others.

Some control, however minor it may seem, *is* critical to human health and well-being. In three nursing-home studies, clients who were given control over when to turn their lights on and off, what time they had meals, and when they made or received telephone calls, showed a reduced mortality rate over eighteen months of more than 50 percent! The implication is that the less control we feel we have, the more we retreat from what seems to be an ambiguous, uncaring world where we don't make a difference. Other studies have concluded that people in secretarial positions, with little or no control over the parameters of their jobs, are far more likely to suffer stress-related illness than executives who may be under constant pressure, but sense some power over the circumstances that affect their destiny.

Unfortunately, the greatest stressor out there is one that we have no control over whatsoever, and IT is driving us nuts. We can't shoot IT, we can't herd IT into a zoo, we can't put papers on the floor for IT, we can't contain IT at all. Oddly enough, we've been dealing with IT since the beginning of time, and pretty effectively, too. But IT mutated on us. IT is CHANGE: rapid, unrelenting, unsettling, uncontrollable CHANGE.

EVERY business conference I attend features an authority on "crisis management" who describes the havoc caused by rapid change. (It's often a speaker I heard giving *exactly the same presentation I heard ten years ago.*)

The philosopher Heraclitus is credited with having said: "The only constant is change." That was the fifth century B.C., and he'd probably read it among graffiti on a temple wall. The oft-stated phrase, "the more things change, the more they stay the same," refers, I think, only to public speakers, politicians, and diapers.

What *is* news is the almost incomprehensible speed of change. In its modern form, change behaves like a rapidly mutating virus. The moment we think we've found an answer, the problem has altered so radically that the cure no longer fits the disease. In the early seventies, Alvin Toffler detailed in *Future Shock* the onset and physical effects of rapid change. "Future shock is no longer a distantly potential danger, but a real sickness from which increasingly large numbers already suffer. It is the disease of change." That was many years ago! I have a new law I call the *Age of Inverse Change:* by the time you understand some new change, the only thing you can be sure of is— you're wrong! In the time it took you to become aware of, comprehend, and respond to the change, IT changed. (That is why we have no spare change.)

Getting tough with change usually doesn't yield impressive results. You can't grab change by the throat, kick it in the head, or kill it with a club. Change will win and you will lose, unless you can learn to lighten up.

The second humor skill—taking yourself lightly and your problems seriously—can help us control what we *can* control—our actions, our reactions, and our attitude.

Aside from trying to "tough it out," a way in which we try to maintain control is by blaming someone or something else for the changes. (Refer back to Chapter 4: "Top Three Warning Signs.") You get angrier at "them" for not fixing things and end up getting more stressed out yourself.

Other common reactions to unpleasant changes are to ignore them, wait for them to pass, or just tune them out.

The Man and the Moon

In 1969, I chose to spend some time with my dad in Northern California. Pop was born in 1900. (I'm not as old as that might imply; he was, uh, quite socially active, you might say, for most of his life.) The difference in our ages made for a relationship that had been awkward and, at times, violent, for most of my life. Because talking only got us into arguments, we usually watched television.

But that day, nearly everyone with a television set was glued to it. The United States had just landed men on the moon for the first time, and they were sending back live pictures of the event. I was engrossed by it all, but Pop didn't seem too interested. As that ghostly and robotic astronaut stepped onto the moon and began his now-famous statement: "That's one small step for a man, one . . . " Dad turned off the set.

"What are you doing?" I asked. "This is one of the greatest events of my life, or yours, for that matter." I headed over to turn the set back on.

"Don't touch the damned thing!" he shouted—his voice grating with anger. He rarely shouted. He rarely showed emotion. I was stunned to turn around and see him wiping a few tears from his cheek.

"Pop," I said quietly, "what's the problem?" I thought, maybe he'd just had too much to drink.

"There were more horses in town than there were cars," he muttered into his half-filled glass of scotch. Then he gazed out the window as if to see a carriage rumbling by.

"I've seen the combustion engine change the world, for God's sake; I worked on cars that could get up hills only in reverse. The planes I worked on were made of canvas and wood and glue."

He went quiet for a moment, grinned at nothing in particular. Then he frowned and poured more scotch into his glass from the half gallon of Black & White that was never more than an arm's length away.

"Damn," he whispered, taking one long gulp from the glass. "I had one of the first radios in the county, one of the fastest cars—a Hupmobile with

huge, wood-spoked wheels. I saw the first movie—
some silent thing about cowboys holding up a train,
and there was a guy playing organ in the orchestra
pit. Got one of the first TVs, too."

He stared up at the ceiling. "But at least those
things gave you some time to get used to 'em. Hell's
bells!"

He pushed himself up from the old leather wing
chair and took a few steps to the window. He finished
his "speech" with his back to me, in a voice so low and
monotonous it made him sound like a man awakened
from a trance.

"It seems like I go to sleep at night and wake up on
another planet. You wanna watch 'em dance on the
moon? Fine. You go ahead. But I've had enough."

He tugged his watch cap on with one hand, grabbed
the half-gallon jug and went out into the yard to work
at something that made sense to him: he was repairing an old car that he intended to give to my sister.
That's where he was when I went to bed.

My last image of him that evening is of a man
dressed in heavy rubber boots, overalls, a torn woolen
shirt, a watch cap pulled over his ears, laboring in a
dim yellow pool of light, hammering and sanding that
old Volkswagen while the moon hung overhead. A
moon I doubt he paused to look up at that night.

After that, he stopped getting out much. He spent
most of his time in the yard, working on one project
or another. He quit watching television entirely and
even his radio was rarely turned on. I don't think I
ever saw him read another newspaper, except when he
wanted to search the classified section for some old
car to restore.

A year later I learned he was the first person in our family to develop cancer. It was an odd variation of the disease, continually producing small clumps of free-floating cancer cells that the doctors removed through tiny incisions in his arms, back, legs, or chest.

I know too much about medicine to assume that Pop's resistance to change and subsequent withdrawal from the world were the only factors that led to his cancer and eventual death. He was, after all, nearly seventy that night when the moon came between us. And although he continued to move and breathe for more than a decade, he quit *living* in 1969 when he closed the door on change.

The 1 Percent Solution

Doctors Vaillant, Selye, Borysenko, and many others have shown us that we *can* adapt to rapid change with fewer devastating consequences, and positively affect our mental and physical health; we *can* remain creative under pressure. We can do so by assuming responsible control of our perspective. How we choose to view challenge and change dictates whether we cope or are crushed.

The second humor skill offers an alternative to toughness, blame, and avoidance in a world of rampaging change: when the going gets tough—the tough lighten up.

As with the other skills in this book, learning to take yourself lightly and your problems seriously may improve your quality of life only a little, but small changes can have great consequences.

If the oxygen content of the atmosphere were decreased by 1 percent, life on earth as we know it would
shut down. If John F. Kennedy had failed to get an
extra 1 percent of the popular vote, he would have lost
the presidency of the United States to Richard Nixon
in 1960. One percent is, after all, the difference between more than half and less than half (say, a wit and
a halfwit).

Humor in Hell

In his *Beyond Survival,* former POW Captain Gerald
Coffee USN [Ret.] tells a story that I found especially
touching. After three months in captivity, Coffee's
Vietnamese jailor ordered him to wash in a rat-infested
shower room littered with rotting bandages and gar-
bage. As he felt the stream of cold water against his
body, Coffee suddenly was overcome with despair.

"And now here I was in this dismal, stinking hole,
body broken, totally uncertain of my future, pressure
to do this, do that, hostility for my daily fare. Men
dying in adjacent cells, my crewman possibly dead.
. . . Finally I raised my head. And there at eye level on
the wall in front of me, scratched indelibly by some
other American who'd been there before me, were the
words, 'Smile, you're on *Candid Camera!*' "

Coffee said he "couldn't not smile." And in that
moment of communion with an unknown ally, "he
laughed out loud, enjoying not only the pure humor
and incongruity of the situation, but also appreciat-
ing the beautiful guy who had mustered the moxie to
rise above his own dejection and frustration and pain
and guilt to inscribe a line of encouragement. . . . "

Hostages in the Middle East, like POWs, have told numerous stories about the importance of humor to hope and survival. Father Lawrence Martin Jenco and David Jacobsen, former hostages in Lebanon, reported that humor helped them maintain their sanity. During their imprisonment, by giving their activities absurd nicknames, they were able to decrease the horror of their position. Morning worship services were referred to as the "Church of the Locked Door," because no one could enter or leave. The hostages called the brackish water they were given "Southern Suburb Chablis."

The potency of humor is nowhere more evident than in a story Father Jenco told a Fort Collins, Colorado, audience in 1987. "Every night," he said, "our captors would ask us what they could get for us. Well, they rarely fulfilled even the simplest request. So, we devised and always responded with one answer in unison. Whenever they asked what we wanted, we replied, 'A taxi.' "

"The night I was released," said Jenco, "the man who had beaten me, spat on me and tormented me for months handed me some money and said softly, 'Here's your two pounds for a taxi, now go home.' "

The man's offer of cabfare clearly tells me that even in hell, bridges can be built, understanding can be realized, respect for adversaries can be maintained, and compassion through humor is part of it all.

RELIEF swept through me in late November 1991 as I sat in a hotel room watching the televised release of hostages Terry Waite and Tom Sutherland. Waite, who'd been working to gain freedom for hostages when he himself was taken prisoner in Lebanon, spent more than five years in captivity. Sutherland was confined for over six years.

News of the hostages' release featured interviews with officials and relatives. Tom Sutherland's brother-in-law, David Murray, made the following remarks to the media: "Tom is a strong guy and he has a tremendous sense of humor. I think anyone with that kind of humor is going to come through a situation like this in good shape." One of Sutherland's first comments to reporters was a bit of good-natured irony on the subject of how long it had taken Waite to negotiate his freedom. Sutherland also talked about the laughter he'd shared with the Syrians transporting him out of captivity, and how, in the first moments of that laughter, he really *knew* he was free.

Tool 1: *Plus Conversation* (or, a Look on the Light Side)

Under far less stressful conditions than the captives faced, many of us exert most of our effort seeking what's broken, paying little attention to what's working. The hostages could have wallowed in their misery. Instead, they disciplined themselves to look for and share any positives they could dredge up from the boredom and loneliness of captivity. Perhaps it was that nobody's teeth had fallen out that day, or they had been served a favorite recipe that they called *hint of chicken*. "That meant," said Father Jenco, "that the chicken had quite recently walked through our rice."

That simple technique—the *plus-conversation*—allowed them to take themselves lightly, and their situation seriously.

The Socket and the Screwball

A young husband, in pursuit of a midnight morsel, entered his darkened kitchen late one night. Several futile flips of the light switch failed to produce illumination—the bulb was burned out. Cursing the darkness, he groped his way to the pantry closet where, by blind trial and error, he found a lightbulb and a stepladder. Hauling the ladder to the middle of the dark room, he overturned a bowl of dry dog food. Crunching the sharp edges of Kibbles and Bits beneath his bare feet added to his mounting irritation. Finally, replacement bulb in one hand, screwdriver in the other, he ascended the stepladder to remove the defunct bulb, and discovered the hard way that a Kibble—or perhaps it was a Bit—had remained stuck to the sole of his foot. As he placed his full weight on that extremity, the pain thus created led to a reflex withdrawal of said foot, a shift in weight, a rather unmanly shriek, and a twisting dive to the tiles below.

At this moment, my wife entered the kitchen and switched on the light over the sink, which I had completely forgotten about.

MORAL: It is better to look for what works before you focus on what's broken.

In your own life, you might try the same *plus-conversation* approach to a bad day or a difficult family problem. What's working? Why? Can you find any way of adapting it to other problem areas? *Plus conversations* are an effective way to start any problem-solving venture. They nourish an environment of *umor,* where spirit and mind are primed for success, creativity, and optimism. They also help us remember to celebrate victories and affirm our capacity for solutions.

Plus Conversation: Step 1

You can practice taking yourself lightly and your challenges seriously right here and now. Write down just one positive thing that has occurred for you in the past twenty-four hours.

Today's Plus Event

Step 2

Tell somebody. Inquire about their *plus events.*

THE *plus-conversation* approach has also been used by corporate clients as a way to keep members of research-and-development teams aiming at solutions instead of each other. But the same principle applies to families, church groups, political campaigns, softball teams . . . whatever.

The next time your group gathers to discuss a problem, have each person come to the meeting with at least one example of something that's going well. If participants can't find something positive in their own department, have them research somebody else's. Perhaps you know how a seemingly unrelated problem within the plant or office was solved. The idea is to come to your problem-solving meetings with the idea that solutions are possible.

Obviously, it is important to know how and why a system, relationship, or product malfunctions so that it can be repaired, but when you begin from a vantage point of success, you are far more likely to be open, hopeful, and creative when it comes to solving problems.

Software Hardball

In spring 1991, J. D. Edwards, an IBM business partner and one of the most successful producers and distributors of software in the world, used the *plus-conversation* technique to solve a product-viability challenge.

I had just addressed a J. D. Edwards users conference in Tampa, Florida. The day after my presentation, people divided into special-interest groups. One group, charged with refining and improving a software package for payroll and personnel, for several weeks prior to the conference had been gathering regularly to discuss a list of more than ninety problems, complaints, and glitches in the system. Their list of troubles had only gotten longer. This time, however, they began the meeting with a list of twenty-one things in the program that were working. That list was followed with a discussion of why those things worked so well, and how they could take lessons from the effective parts of the program, apply them to the problem areas, and focus on the most important elements to be solved.

It was terrifically satisfying for me to watch the good humor, laughter, and whirl of solutions which evolved in that meeting. Occasionally, clients will ignore a concept like *plus-conversations* because it seems too simple. The folks at J. D. Edwards could not be leaders in their field, with a 300 percent growth rate over the past three years, without being open to new ideas and approaches. They are fortunate in that the tyranny of Terminal Professionalism has never been allowed to get a stranglehold on that company.

Tool 2: *Minivacations*

Although Mideast hostages Tom Sutherland and Terry Anderson were kept like "rabbits in a box" in small, windowless rooms, and were regularly subjected to mock executions staged by their captors, they allowed themselves to play. They devised chess pieces out of tinfoil bits left from cheese wrappings; they made playing cards from well-worn book pages.

As often as possible, the men would lead each other on imaginary walks, pacing in small circles, with their eyes closed. Sutherland, born in Scotland, would lead Anderson on fantasy tours across the moors. Anderson, an American who had worked in Japan, described in minute detail the temples and shrines he had seen in Tokyo. The men would smile, laugh, or let out a sigh of appreciation as they "looked" with inward vision upon the beauty of a scene one of them had described. The trips often lasted more than an hour, ending with imaginary feasts on favorite foods.

Like the hostages, you and I can remember our right to play. Or, when play isn't practical, we can use our imagination to take minivacations that dilute stress. These mental quick trips are inexpensive, require no advance booking, and you can always drink the water. From hundreds of client suggestions I've chosen just a few that I hope will trigger your own investigation of this simple tool.

Batter Up! Ned, a physical therapist, had one of the most unusual minivacations I know of. Although he loved his work, many of his clients were severely ill, depressed, and emotionally demanding. He says, "Sometimes, the combination of bureaucratic inefficiency and the terrible pain of my patients was more than I could tolerate. I found myself becoming less and less effective at my job, and thinking more often of quitting."

After attending a humor seminar, he decided to design his own minivacation. "I immediately remembered how much I used to love to play softball," he said. "I decided to integrate that memory into my work a few times a day. The result was wacky, but effective.

"I set up a sort of adult T-ball game in my office. It was just a heavy metal stand with a variable-height shaft. I could adjust the shaft from about knee level to shoulder level. Then I got one of those lightweight, plastic balls—you know, the kind with the holes in it? And I got the closest thing I could find to a regulation-size bat, made of plastic. Several times a day, when I feel myself tightening up or getting frustrated, I just step into my office, put that ball on the shaft, and hit about a dozen quick home runs as hard as I can."

Ned's conclusion? "It really helps! Of course, it helped even more when I put a picture of my congressman on the ball."

Fear and Flying: Mental imagery has tremendous power to relieve fear—even when it borders on phobia. A friend who flies a lot but hates it, especially the takeoff, lightens up by mentally focusing on his greatest joy—his son. As the engines roar he imagines special moments from the boy's childhood, then mentally projects this young life into the future. By the time the wheels lift off the ground my friend says he is beyond relaxed, he's blissful. The technique works so well, the imagery is so enjoyable, that he says he now sort of looks forward to the intensity of blasting down the runway.

"The fact is that the body cannot tell the difference between what is actually happening and what you are imagining," says author Joan Borysenko in *Minding the Body, Mending the Mind.* "When you consider all the negative fantasies that run through the mind each day, it's no wonder that the body stores so much tension. Why not purposely substitute positive fantasies by actively guiding your imagination?"

Cop Rocks: During a year-long series of *Humor Option* trainings for the Boulder, Colorado, Police Training Academy, one officer I'll call Don came up with a minivacation that helped him moderate the daily stresses in his administrative duties.

Don was an ardent scuba diver who spent every possible vacation with his family at one dive site or another. After attending the workshop, he went to his collection of stones and shells that he'd gathered over the years. Choosing one item from each place in which he'd been diving, he placed them in a leather pouch that he carried with him.

"If I'm having one of those days," he told me, "when I think that the bad guys are bound to win, or that some rotten cop will stink up the whole profession, I force myself to stop, take a breath, and open that pouch. I just take a few seconds to select one of the stones or shells and look at it. I remember the trip, the water conditions, the moment when my family and I discovered a piece of coral or an exotic fish that excited us. It's the damnedest thing, but that few seconds reminds me to take myself lightly and my work seriously. I might open the pouch once a week or once an hour on some days. I don't know why it works, but it does. I just mellow out and get back to work. At the end of the tough days, I'm a lot less tense and crazed."

Unclogged Dancing: "Perhaps you aren't familiar with clog dancing," the letter began. The woman who wrote me this wonderful letter also introduced me to one of the most peculiar minivacations I'd heard of.

"But I've been competing in clog-dancing contests for nearly twenty years, and I just love it. A friend from the city who witnessed clog dancers for the first time told me it looked like a group of exterminators in wooden shoes who were trying to stomp a million bugs to death in ten seconds."

You have to understand that often no music is played at clog-dancing events, and so when you close your eyes it sounds like a hundred carpenters trying to drive in the same nail; sometimes they bash each others' fingers, which leads to a series of whoops, hollers, and "wahoos." Got it?

Ms. Clog was a nurse who worked the exceptionally stressful night shift in a big-city hospital emergency room. She carried a small tape recorder that clipped to her belt, and had an earplug speaker line. Between emergencies, or while doing paperwork, she would listen to an audio tape of a clog-dancing concert. It left one ear open for her to hear calls on the loudspeaker, a phone ringing, or some unfortunate with an icepick in his head howling for help from the parking lot.

"I don't know if you have any idea how intense and nerve-wracking my kind of work can be," she wrote. "But since I started taking minivacations to my clog-dancing contests every few hours, I really have been able to stay more relaxed and less frantic. It's not a scientific test, but I find that my blood pressure and heart rate actually drop after just a few seconds of listening to the tape. I let one of the physicians listen to it, but he said it sounded like gunfire in an asylum, and it made him nervous. Clog dancing is an acquired taste, I guess."

I guess.

The point is that minivacations can take any number of creative forms, from an audio cassette to a poster, a photo, or a leather pouch filled with rocks and shells. The idea simply is to take yourself lightly a few times every day. Here are just a few more client-suggested minivacations.

- A neurosurgeon listens to country and western music while he operates. (Do-si-do, swing your scalpel to and fro.)

- A humor consultant tacks photos of trophy-sized trout to his office bulletin board.

- A plant manager has a photo enlarged to two feet by three feet and hangs it over her desk, covered by a small curtain. When she wants to take a minivacation, she draws back the curtain and gazes at the pristine Swiss lake as if it were just outside the door.

- A saleswoman carries a sachet filled with cedar chips that she collected at her favorite forest retreat. "Every time I open my briefcase," she told me, "the scent of cedar triggers all the good feelings I associate with British Columbia."

Take just a moment and write down your own ideas for a minivacation. Then try one of them out for a few weeks and see if it helps.

Tool 3: *Zygo Boogie*

Yes, the final tool in enlarging our capacity to take self lightly and challenge seriously, is yet another Humaerobic exercise. This is really one of my favorites and serves a variety of purposes, as I will explain.

The Zygo Boogie was developed in association with my first partner in this work, Christian Hageseth III, M.D. In exploring the physiology of laughter itself, we noticed that almost everyone went through exactly the same muscular processes when they laughed. Although the entire series of events takes less than a second when triggered in natural circumstances, we've broken it down so that you can more fully appreciate and experience each phase and actually practice the natural, physiological process of laughter. Don't expect to end up in hysterics every time—you won't. But as you become more adept with the Zygo Boogie, you will begin to notice the various stages when you

laugh naturally; the result is that most people experience more intense and enjoyable laughter. Ready?

1. Grin a Little Grin: You do this exercise by contracting the zygomaticus major—the primary smiling muscle, which runs from your cheekbones to the corners of your mouth. Don't let the eyes, eyebrows, or cheeks get involved. Just let the corners of the mouth barely turn upward. If you're looking in a mirror, you'll notice that this grin, without other expression, is what we commonly call an "insincere smile." You've seen it, usually accompanying a line like "Of course we'll consider a raise," or "Yeah, Mom and Dad, I love going to the ballet with you guys."

So, grin, release. Grin and release. Grin, release. Got it? Good. Next . . .

2. Squint a Little Squint: You know, this brings a touch of sincerity to a smile—"a twinkle to the eyes." By slightly contracting the orbicularis oculi—the fine sheath of muscles around the eyes—you get a little crinkle at the outer edge. That's where "laugh lines" form, ideally, over the years. The eyes narrow just a bit, but the brows don't move yet.

Squint, release. Squint, release. Squint, release. Good. Now, do steps one and two slowly. Grin . . . Squint. Relax. Grin . . . Squint . . . Relax. (A woman told me that this sounded like an exercise in a Lamaze class for clowns.)

3. Raise the Frontalis: Ah, the frontalis muscle. One of my favorites. The forehead—which, for bald guys like myself, extends nearly to the back of my neck—

rises. Your forehead wrinkles a bit and your eyebrows bob upward. Let's try it.

Raise, hold, relax. Raise, hold, relax. Raise, hold, and . . . relax.

All together now, from the beginning.

Grin, squint, raise the frontalis. Hold (not easy to squint and raise your eyebrows at the same time, is it?) and relax. Repeat a few times until you've got it.

4. Tighten the Platysma: That's right, the set of muscles in the lower face and neck that, when contracted, expose the bottom teeth, as in: "*Yes, I can handle it!*" (tighten the platysma). Practice a few contractions and releases of the the platysma. Now, from the top.

Grin . . . Squint . . . Forehead up . . . Platysma tightens . . . (Get a load of this one in a mirror. It's a great face to use when you want to get a waiter's attention.)

Repeat three times. Relax. Remember, this isn't stupid, it's _____?

4½. Involuntary: This intermediate muscle involvement is actually involuntary, and is the first major muscle group, outside of the face, to get involved just prior to the vocalization we call laughter. What happens, essentially, is that the anal sphincter muscle tightens. Pay attention the next time you laugh out loud, and you'll feel a contraction sort of, uh, sneaking up behind you. This is an automatic response and need not be practiced, but I thought you'd like to know.

(A minister friend insists that this muscle contraction proves that God is a great engineer. "After all," he says, "if that muscle didn't tighten, nobody would laugh!")

5. The Belly Laugh: Place your hand on your tummy. Now, breathe in and out, using your diaphragm; if you're successful, the tummy will expand as you breathe in, and flatten—or attempt to flatten—when you breathe out.

Draw the breath in by expanding the tummy. Now, exhale sharply while emitting a high-pitched "ha" sound. Ha! Got it? Good. Now, repeat a dozen times very rapidly: Breath in, tummy distends, sharp breath out, and "Ha!" Breath in, breath out, and "Ha?" Ha! Ha! Ha! Ha! Ha! Ha! Ha!

How ya doin'? Ready to put them all together? Here we go.

Grin. Squint. Forehead up. Platysma contracts. Now, using the belly breath, let out a series of ha's!

6. Rocking Movement: Observe your friends when they laugh heartily, or look around the next time you attend a performance by stand-up comics. When people *really* get to laughing hard, they start rocking back and forth. Why? Because laughter relaxes all the major muscle groups in the body, and you start rocking back and forth as the muscles in the thoracic region begin relaxing and contracting.

Practice just rocking back and forth in your chair. Simple. Now, once more, put the entire series together.

Grin. Squint. Forehead up. Platysma contracts. Belly laughter. Rocking motion. Keep going for a few seconds until you've got it all working.

7. Contact! You know this one. As laughter intensifies, we need to physically express it by pounding the table, slapping our knee(s) or clapping our hands together.

Why? Beats me. Speaking of beating, some of us get so carried away we begin to slap or slug our friends. This is most often a pleasant exchange. Although, when I go to comic performances with my wife, I prefer that someone sit between us; otherwise, I leave the concert covered with black-and-blue "happy bruises." This one's simple, and so let's just add it to the progression. Here we go again.

Grin. Squint. Forehead up! Platysma tightens. Belly laughter begins. Start rocking back and forth, at the same time slapping your knee(s), pounding a table, whacking a friend.

Whew. Almost done.

8. Tears: Yes, tears. "I laughed until I cried" is one of the pleasantest experiences our body can give us. Of course, you can't make yourself cry tears of hysterical, laughing joy on command. But, the next time you start to laugh, you can experiment by being aware of which step you level off at, and choosing to intensify the experience by adding one more. For instance, if you're grinning and squinting, just add the forehead; or, if you're laughing, start rocking back and forth a bit. And when you do have those wonderful moments of laughing until you cry, remember this exercise and it will put you right over the edge.

If you choose to do the Humaerobics exercises regularly, make sure you include the Zygo Boogie. Like all the humor exercises, the effects are usually intensified if you do them with even a small group. But they are useful in solo situations as well. According to one client, if you practice this exercise in a public restroom, you're guaranteed to have the place all to yourself.

Take Yourself Lightly and Your Humor Exercises Seriously

Before we head into Chapter 6 and the final humor skill, I want to reaffirm what we're about with all this silliness.

The simple act of practicing any of the suggested tools, from Photo Funnies to the Zygo Boogie, affirms that you care enough about yourself to "play" toward enjoying life more. It takes time for these exercises to have an effect, so please relax and enjoy yourself. That's an order.

On his way to Diego's, Jeffrey discovers a woman harmed by information excess. . . . A small crowd has collected around her, listening to her complicated monologue: Birds of Prey Cards, sunspot soufflé, Antarctic unemployment.
—*Ted Mooney,* Easy Travel to Other Planets

6. Misery and Pain Are Free, but Joy Has a Price

Easy to Say, Hard to Do

A disciplined sense of **joy in being alive** is the third humor skill. How, I wonder, does something as basic and desirable as joy in being alive come to be thought of as unprofessional, childish, or simpleminded? For many people, antijoy attitudes are established early in life. Oh, I know. At one time it sounded simpleminded to me, too. And it's far easier to talk about a sense of joy than to cultivate one.

The **Directory of Positive Attitude Platitudes** is full of glib sayings about staying cheerful to combat every misfortune from acne to armed robbery. At one time or another we've all been liberally dosed with this cheerful advice:

Don't worry. Be Happy!
Every cloud has a silver lining.
When life gives you lemons, make lemonade.

> Laugh and the world laughs with you, cry
> and you cry alone.

(Did you repress an urge to smack the advice giver with a fresh, forty-pound flounder?)

Advice givers mean well, but they often ignore the value of working through and learning from pain and loss. Perhaps they don't want to deal with pain themselves, but would rather bury it under a bushel of surface brightness, positive thinking and self-help slathering.

GROWING up in an alcoholic environment, I had the mistaken perception that a sense of joy in life somehow betrayed the pain of those around me. If I was feeling good and my family wasn't, something was wrong with me.

Even if you weren't subjected to that kind of antijoy training, we're all brought up with contradictory messages about the value of fun in life. Most of us recall our parents telling us to "Sit still" and to "Get serious." Or teachers who barked, "Wipe that stupid smile off your face!" In my family, the popular wisdom was that by being tougher than everyone else, we'd end up "winners." Luck and mental toughness would lead to our survival, success, and manhood. That brand of manhood, of course, was the kind in the movies—Clint Eastwood or John Wayne, *not* Woody Allen.

Being funloving and lighthearted, on the other hand, was associated with weakness or drunkenness.

This was all a dangerous lie. In fact, losing the sense of joy in being alive is one of the first indicators of mental illness—as of much physical illness. Those with a strong will to live consistently discipline themselves to nurture the positives life has to offer.

What Is Real? Really?

A sense of joy may sound abstract or too "unrealistic" to be regarded as a humor skill. The fact is, our society has a bias against too much optimism and happiness in people who *ought* to be miserable. Focusing on the good in life, or assuming the best outcome—when illness or some other catastrophe makes living difficult—often sounds dangerously like "not facing up to reality" for those of us who learned that "denial (of external reality)," or *delusion,* is a defense mechanism characterizing major psychosis.

You can hear plenty of nervous laughter about delusions, the specialty of schizophrenics and paranoids (such as, I am the King of Mars or Mick Jagger's ex-girlfriend, or that Chef Paul has a secret plot to steal my recipes). Rather than indulge in self-delusion, we take the grimmest view of *reality.* "Let's look at this realistically," usually means, "Let's think about the worst aspect of this person, place, thing, or situation."

Recent evidence, however, indicates that "realism," when it happens to be pessimistic, can adversely affect mental health. Robert Ornstein, Ph.D., and David Sobel, M.D., point out in their *Healthy Pleasures* that most people see themselves as happier and more competent than the average individual—which is, of course, a statistical impossibility. Despite their "unrealistic" view such individuals, say the authors, are well adjusted and healthy.

Ornstein and Sobel go on to explain that people with a more accurate self-assessment "will often openly admit such things as 'My boss doesn't trust me,' 'My husband believes I am lazy,' 'My wife thinks I am stingy.' For this select community, negative statements regarding themselves correspond well to others' judgments. These men and women are realistic. They know they're not respected and that others don't like them, and they're right. As you may guess by now, these are the people who are either mildly depressed or are on their way to a depression."

There is, it seems, such a thing as "positive illusion." After considering "mountains" of research, Shelley E. Taylor, Ph.D., of UCLA, and Jonathon D. Brown, Ph.D., of Southern Methodist University, conclude that well-being depends almost completely upon the individual's "illusions of overly positive self-evaluation, exaggerated perceptions of control or mastery, and unrealistic optimism."

Positive illusions, according to Taylor and Brown, "are not only characteristic of normal human thought but are also necessary to meet the usual criteria for mental health: the ability to care about others, to be content, and to work productively." The researchers noticed that "people who score the highest on tests of self-deception (that is, they deny ever having threatening but universal feelings such as guilt) score lowest on measures of psychopathology and depression."

Evidently, then, a positive focus, even when it means we're "out of touch with reality," can directly or indirectly shift the odds in our favor. But this third humor skill is far more than attitudinal. Action is crucial to the strength and effectiveness of a disciplined sense of joy in being alive.

Joy Is Action

Although most of us think of happiness as something that falls randomly at our feet, a sense of joy in being alive can and should be based in direct action. We can deliberately discover the things that nourish and sustain our sense of fun, laughter, and humor and let them strengthen us. Joy in being alive allows those who possess it to draw strength from circumstances that would defeat other people.

During his seven years of imprisonment in North Vietnam, Captain Gerald Coffee maintained control of his perspective by nourishing his sense of joy. Rather than focus on what he didn't have, he sought refuge in structuring a daily routine, which included **taking responsibility for his own entertainment.** Coffee sang all the songs he had ever known, "categorizing them, dwelling upon the memories specific to each." He became a naturalist, studying "the rats, the cockroaches, the ants, flies and mosquitoes; watching and learning the habits of the little tropical lizards called geckos."

Even when he was denied the most basic of human necessities, he called upon his creative strength to find some meaning in the journey. During the dark days of imprisonment, he reflected upon his values and beliefs and, remarkably, grew stronger. "This is not to say that the loneliness and boredom weren't nearly overwhelming sometimes," Coffee writes in *Beyond Survival,* "but I was gradually learning how to deal with them."

Captain Coffee's story once again shows the value of *umor*—fluidity and adaptability. When the going gets tough, the tough lighten up and live, rather than tighten up and lose.

The Antijoy Shtick

It isn't only childhood training and adult trauma that threaten to rob us of happiness. Our joy in life can also be distorted by a dominantly adult

condition known as CNNility—pronounced *CNNility.*
In the high-minded circles I frequent, it's called JUNC
(*J*umbled, *U*nfiltered, *N*ews *C*rap).

Known for its focus on what's bad, broken, and battered, JUNC can erode our sense of joy in being alive
as surely as any imprisonment, disease, or battering.
And JUNC has expanded crazily in the past few decades.

In fact, JUNC reached a twentieth-century apex—
or, nadir, depending upon your viewpoint—with the
now historic combat for Kuwait called Desert Storm.
For weeks the media, from international television to
local sales circulars and even the comic strips, were
awash in observations, guesses, interpretations, sati-
rizations, patriotic support, and patriotic protest. The
world focused around the clock on a conflict in which
news reporters appeared to outnumber troops. The
world watched . . . and watched . . . and watched.

Even now, JUNC-ies and channel grazers, rather
than choose their pleasures, automatically hook the
TV-IV into their brain and subject themselves to a
constant drip of unfiltered info-JUNC for hours at a
time. Between September 1990 and August 1991 the
average American, according to A. C. Nielsen, watched
six hours and fifty-six minutes of television a day. The
result of these transfusions is *information angst,* a
condition that erodes joy in being alive through obsessive indulgence in JUNC *reality.*

In March 1991, as Desert Storm winds continued
blowing, Roma and I were on tour in Australia. As
most ninth-graders know (if they were educated
somewhere other than in the United States), Australia
is sixteen hours ahead of the U.S.A.'s Pacific Standard
Time Zone. Every night, anxious Australians would

tune in to yesterday's news—which was, of course, today's news Down Under—coverage of what had happened the day before yesterday, today, in the Mideast.

There I was, along with my Aussie mates, watching the morning news from midnight to three or four A.M., staggering off to bed and rising a few hours later to bemoan the state of the world. My sense of joy in being alive took a sharp plunge. The humor seminars I was presenting began to seem less meaningful; I wondered if my upcoming trout-fishing trip to Tasmania was frivolous as I watched SMART bombs blowing up stupid buildings, women and men dying, political leaders bombasting one another, fires and oil slicks destroying the land and sea over which we fought. The more I watched, the more obsessed I became. And angry. I wondered why I had ever imagined that much of anything was funny.

My wife, noticing my mood change, looked up from her reading and calmly offered a solution: "Turn off the television, and go for a walk by the sea."

"What?" I asked incredulously. "And miss . . . miss . . . I dunno, miss something important?"

"Oh right," she said, " I forgot that you were waiting for a call from Stormin' Norman. He wanted your advice on the next bombing run over Ryadh."

Her subtle sarcasm was not lost on me. "We'll go for a walk by the ocean as soon as this interview is over."

She glanced at the set. "Who's being interviewed?"

I shrugged. By now CNN had interviewed everyone who had ever been to Kuwait, heard of Kuwait, or held the belief that Kuwait was a fuzzy green fruit from New Zealand. I believe this fellow was a psychologist from some local junior college who had gotten "K-U-W-A-I-T" right in a spelling bee twenty years

ago. Whatever . . . his comments have stayed with me
(more or less).

Q. You believe, do you not, that the constant news
coverage of the war is having detrimental effects on
the populace?

A. Inundated is not informed. I doubt that most people understand what they're watching anyway. I do
believe that this constant attention to violent and negative action distorts people's view of reality. As they
focus on what's wrong with the world, and how powerless they are to do anything but watch the horror
unfold, that perspective dominates other areas of
their lives. Everything gets worse, or seems to. It's unhealthy.

Q. I'm not sure I agree with you, but what would you
suggest to those people who do find some sense in
what you're saying?

[The psychologist paused for a moment, staring upward as though waiting for inspiration. The camera
zoomed in as he turned toward it and said:]

A. Turn off your television set, now. Go do something
that puts you in touch with the people you love and
care about. Tune in to the news once a week, once a
day, for a few minutes at the most. You'll be amazed by
the fact that events seem to proceed with or without
your constant attention. Turn it off.

Q. Thank you very much for your comments. Now,
it's time for an update from Saudi Arabia.

I started to laugh. I rocked in my chair and slapped
my leg. "That's great!" I shrieked.

Roma looked at me quizzically.

"Don't you get it?" I managed to choke out between
fits of laughter. "I had to watch television to hear

some guy tell me to stop watching television! I mean, I wouldn't have known I shouldn't watch if I hadn't been watching!"

After convincing Roma that I didn't need oxygen or a tight white jacket, I unplugged the television set, and together we went for a long walk on the beach. That was the last time I watched news coverage of the war for more than thirty minutes a day. I overheard everything else I needed to know from conversations in restaurants, in cabs, and even walking along the beach. When people asked me how I felt about the war, I would say, "The same way I do about the next one."

Most people would leave me alone, no doubt pitying me for my obvious lack of patriotism, intelligence, or funds to buy a TV set. But I no longer had to ask myself, "Is there any meaning or purpose in doing humor seminars when the world is in such pain?" The answer was obvious: there's never been more need for a sense of joy in being alive than there is now.

If we do not generate and practice reverence for the joys of life, then the miseries, wars, and backed-up septic tanks will pull us under. We're likely to become the kind of people who make me saddest: those whose attitude is, "Let's get what we can for ourselves and get out while the getting is good." Those are not the people who will help solve our problems. The problem solvers, I'm convinced, are the ones who love it here so much they just can't stand to see it all go down the drain.

One of the most effective techniques for creating that vital sense of joy in life was suggested to me by one of the young people I worked with through a hospice program.

The Gift of Joy

Chuck was thirteen when he came home from the hospital, not because he was getting better, but because he wanted to be with the people he knew and loved when he died. A nurse was on duty to help with medications, and I came by the house to visit with him and his family several times a week. On most of my visits, Chuck was unconscious or groggy from the heavy intravenous doses of morphine he was given for pain control. But the last time I saw him alive he was awake and remarkably lucid.

"I got something for you." He reached under his pillow and withdrew a rolled-up, somewhat crumpled sheaf of papers. "I want you to give this to my mom 'n' dad after I die. You'll know when it's right, I guess. Will you?"

"What is it?" I asked.

"It's a list of all the fun we had, all the times we laughed."

I almost gasped in amazement. With all the fear and anger and disappointment he had every right to be feeling, here he was trying to to look out for his parents.

"Like what?" I asked feebly, trying to regain my composure.

Chuck grinned, and launched into a story I wouldn't have thought he had the strength to tell.

"Like, the time Mom and Dad and Chrissie and Linda and me were dressed up as those guys in the Fruit of the Loom underwear ad, and Dad's driving us to a costume party. Dad was a bunch of grapes and I was an apple, and the others were different things like bananas and stuff? And Dad gets pulled over for speeding. When the policewoman came up to the car she looked in and just started laughin', really hard. I mean, she could hardly stand up, ya know? And we all started laughing and the cop said: 'Where you all headed—a salad bar?' Dad said he was sorry to be speeding, but his kids were getting so ripe that they were starting to draw flies. And the cop laughed till she had to take off her dark glasses and wipe tears from her eyes, and she said: 'Well, get out of here, but go slow, I don't want to find you squashed all over the highway.' "

Chuck laughed, and so did I. Later that night I looked over the pages to see a list that included Disneyland, horseback riding, camping, the speeding-fruit story, and others, some of which made me laugh out loud. What an incredible gift, I thought. The list ended with a note from Chuck to his parents.

"I know you're real upset right now that I'm going away, but I don't want you to forget this stuff. I don't want you to just remember me being skinny and sick. Think about these things, too, because this is what I remember most."

A Joy List

Nearly ten years after I'd met and said goodbye to Chuck, and had begun doing humor seminars, I realized that I had never taken the time to list the things that really nourished and sustained my own sense of joy in being alive. When I tried to make my own Joy List, I found out why I'd been avoiding the task: I couldn't remember much. Chuck's list took up both sides of six pages; mine was done in three lines. I could bulk up my Joy List if I added all the things

I wanted to do, but didn't have time for, or all the things I used to do, but was "too grown up for." I decided to start over.

On my first list were:

1. Making love with my wife.
2. Camping.
3. Fishing.

It didn't take much imagination to see that I couldn't do any of those three things at the office; at least, not without getting in a lot of trouble. If those were the only things that I could think of, I was liable to wear out my gear long before I wore out my interest. (I refer, of course, to my fishing and camping gear.)

The idea of a Joy List is so simple that some of you may disregard it as a serious tool for building resilience in life. Remember, though, if it seems *silly,* it's probably a blessing.

The first step was to get a pocket-size note pad and carry it with me. Whenever I saw, heard about, or experienced something that made me smile, laugh, or just feel good, I wrote it down. It wasn't easy at first. I wasn't used to looking for the things in life that made me feel good; I was far more likely to spend time complaining about or avoiding things that made me feel bad.

I was surprised to find that years later, after asking my audiences to take five minutes and start a Joy List, most people over thirty could not come up with more than a half-dozen items. Evidently, I wasn't the only human being who had bought into the idea that realistic, professional, and adult meant serious, uptight, and grouchy.

I started looking for the moments of absurdity, laughter, and joy in and around me. The list grew:

- Simply taking a short walk after lunch. It made me feel better, and so it went on the list.

- During my lecture tours I began stopping in at little stationery shops in different cities and towns to browse through the humorous greeting cards. I would select one and send it to myself back home with the words, "Glad you were here, hope you're there." I started a collection of those cards that now fills an entire file drawer.

- Going to drive-in movies with my wife. As those pits of pubescent passion are disappearing from the American landscape, Roma and I look for them wherever we travel. Our attendance is a vote of support for what is, sadly, a vanishing view of life. A drive-in, glowing like an alien spacecraft hidden in the tall cornfields of Iowa, will draw us like a beacon.

- Teaching our black Labrador retriever, Gracie, to walk backward. It hasn't been easy, but it will be worth it one day when I demonstrate her retrieving skills for one of my bird-hunting friends. I'll tell Gracie to sit and stay, then I'll throw the ball and give her the hand signal to back up. As the ball heads east, and Gracie backpedals furiously westward, I'll tell my perplexed comrade, "Try not to laugh at her, she's dyslexic." Just the thought of pulling this one off makes it Joy List material.

After eight years, my Joy List has nearly three hundred headings where once were only three. The original three are still there, of course—right at the top. My perfect day would still be spent lying on the banks of some isolated river in New Zealand, holding Roma in one arm while casting for trout with my other. Ahhhhhh. Perfection.

This is all it takes to start a Joy List: a pocket memo pad; a pen, pencil, or crayon; and the willingness to watch for or create new moments of joy, laughter, and play for yourself that you can write down.

For the Joy List to be truly effective, you have to *really* make the list, not just think about making it. Honoring and respecting yourself enough to write those things down is essential to the success of this technique. It is, perhaps, the simplest tool we offer for humor skill development, and one of the most effective.

If mentally practicing the elements that sustain a sense of joy in being alive can help people like Captain Coffee and Chuck, then it follows that physically pursuing joyful activities might have an even greater benefit for the rest of us. Don't buy it until you try it—but please, try it. For those of you with a strong tendency to procrastinate, how about making use of the blank space here—**now**!

1.

2.

3.

4.

5.

6.

And so on . . .

Learn to Play

Lao Tzu, or some other inscrutable Easterner, said that a truly successful person is one who can sit on the banks of a river, doing nothing and enjoying it. (He did not imply, however, that this was the only activity that occupied a successful person's time—just some of it.)

Before I could do nothing and enjoy it, however, I had to learn to play. Play is the first step toward complete relaxation, total comfort, absolute abandonment of control, and the ability to just be in the world without wanting to run it. In other words, play is the first step to peace of mind, spirit, and heart.

Many of my clients have no idea what the word *play* means. Oh, they say to me, "Yessir, Mr. Metcalf, I agree with what you're saying, 110 percent; I work hard and I *play* hard."

I cringe when I hear that statement, and I feel compelled to let them in on a secret that completely confuses them: play is not supposed to be hard; that's why they call it *play*.

I cannot, for example, call the games of golf that most amateurs pursue, *play*. When I'm out on the links with clients who throw clubs, holler, swear, and damn those little dimpled, white balls to sizzle in hell, it doesn't sound like play. The truth is, most of us can't tell the difference between play and competition.

Participating in competition is a healthy human endeavor. I enjoy competing myself, but I don't call it play. Play means, simply, that nobody wins or loses. People play just to have fun, no matter what the outcome. For most of us, then, play has to be a solo activity in the beginning because we are so used to wanting to beat someone, or win at something, or stand out from the crowd, that we can turn even the most playful activities into stress-expanding madness. Next, some suggestions on learning to play— not for *you* of course, because I'm sure *you* know how to play. But perhaps these ideas will help a friend.

Learn to juggle. There are many places to start. A workshop with Steve Allen, Jr., for example, will leave you a master of juggling cheesecloth scarves. Or you can seek out one of my favorite books, *Juggling for the Complete Klutz*. To begin, just set aside a few moments a week for practicing your juggling. The moment you notice yourself tightening up, swearing, or trying REALLY HARD to juggle perfectly, quit. Learning to play shouldn't be hard.

Take a mime, clown, or acting class. Make it clear to your teacher that you aren't interested in becoming a professional, but rather, you want to learn to have fun. If the instructor seems confused by this concept, find another instructor, or go back to juggling.

When you're ready for some group activities, you might want to order the book *A Bag of Tricks,* by Jane Sanborn. Jane helps manage one of the more creative training environments I know of at the Colorado Outdoor Education Center in Florrisant, Colorado. For almost fifty years, her parents, Sandy and Laura Sanborn, along with their extended family of sons, daughters, grandkids, in-laws, and assorted friends, have become adept at helping children and adults learn to love, play, and work upon our planet.

A classic book about the power of play is *Playfair: Everybody's Guide to Noncompetitive Play* by the modern progenitors of purposeful play, Matt Weinstein and Joel Goodman. Along with fun and philosophy are directions for more than fifty cooperative games, plus practical information on community, family, and corporate team-building. The authors believe that healthy play teaches people to make appropriate choices between competition and cooperation. And, as they note: "Cooperation is a matter of survival. The real world faces . . . significant problems and crises that can *only* be solved through cooperation."

Once you've learned to play for the sheer pleasure of it, you might be ready to do *nothing* for the same reason.

Doing *nothing* isn't as scary as it sounds. I had to start with sixty seconds a day, in the morning, before I was too awake to consider all that had to be done in the ensuing eighteen hours. My first nothing game was to lie in bed after the alarm went off and stare at the ceiling. On my best mornings, I even thought about *nothing*. It was hard. My mind, my training, and my ego all nagged at me to get on with the important business of my life. After only a few days, though, the morning minute became tremendous fun. I was awake and aware and empty. It was energizing.

As time went on I was able to expand my zone-out time to three- or even five-minute periods. I would lie on the front lawn after returning home from the office, close my eyes, rest my head on my briefcase, and listen to the birds muttering in the trees. Eventually, I was able to spend an entire day swaying in a friend's hammock. I still remember watching sunlight patterns change in the treetops between drowsy periods of fantasy and sleep, listening to the lap of waves against the lakeshore and the ducks paddling by. (Unfortunately, I've felt so guilty ever since, I've avoided taking more than a few minutes a day of doing nothing. I still have to work on this one. Write and let me know how it works out for you.)

If doing nothing makes you uneasy, get up and play for a while, then lie down and try once more to empty your mind. This exercise drives some people— my wife, for one—absolutely fruit-loopie, so be cautious. You might want to wait until a few weeks into your pursuit of humor before trying this one. (If I don't hear from you, I'll assume you've succeeded.)

The Weekends Only Calendar

Do you have a daily planner? You know, one of those thick little "pocket-size" packages that allows you to divide your life into hours and seconds so that you can cram as much as possible into every day. Of course, you do. Either that, or you keep several calendars that mark off how you will divide your years, your months, your days, and your hours. Can you remember a period in your life when the primary divisions were the seasons? No? Then you're younger than I am—or you weren't paying attention.

I distinctly recall the year 1959. That was the year they built the largest Cadillac ever: twenty-one feet of steel, glass, leather, rubber, and FINS! My dad had one. (I think he won it in a poker game because in scripted, ornate, white letters on the rear quarter-panel, he had written: *Full Boat—Aces High*.)

In 1959 there were no seconds, minutes, hours or even days of division *for me*. I was fourteen years old.

There was summer—ahhhh: fishing, baseball, fishing, playing, and fishing.

There was fall: school started, fishing was good and special because it consumed only the weekends instead of entire weeks.

There was winter: Thanksgiving, Christmas, New Year's Day, and, of course, some ice fishing. (They call it ice fishing, by the way, because ice is sometimes all you catch.)

And there was spring: great fishing, baseball, and the promise of summer looming on a fragrant horizon.

That was 1959.

As I write this, it is spring 1991. My time is now broken into hours, minutes, seconds. This abuse of time reached a zenith for me three years ago when my pocket calendar makers sent me the notice that it was time to purchase another year of tiny spaces to cram full of really important things to do.

Opening up my new January calendar, I was so startled that I actually let out a little gasp of fright: the weekends were getting smaller!

I quickly riffled through the other pages, the other months, and it was the same throughout the year! Oh, God, help me! The weekends are melting!

In a brief moment of rational thought, I remembered that the people who make my pocket calendar don't own time; they just parcel it out to idiots like me. I was furious. What right did they have to make the days of the work week larger, and the weekends smaller? I checked with several friends who use the same calendar. I thought, perhaps it was a personal attack; but no, they had all suffered the same fate: wimpy weekends, wordlessly whispering their wispy way into the twilight zone of time. Remembering the words of the Chinese philosopher about success, I rebelled.

I went to a stationery store and bought the largest wall calendar I could find. Back at home, my wife, who is used to such odd bursts of behavior, watched in silence as I neatly scissored out Monday through Friday, leaving Friday night, Saturday, and Sunday intact.

Triumphant, I taped my tattered flag of rebellion to the refrigerator door. For all the fervor that went into it, I had to agree with Roma when she said: "That's really ugly, Charley. Either we improve the appearance or it goes in your office."

It was not really a suggestion. Shortly thereafter C.W. Metcalf & Company began to produce and market a more attractive version of the **Weekends Only Calendar**, or WOC, as it has been dubbed. You can create your own model or order one of ours. Either way, this is how the WOC touchstone works.

The WOC is a simple but effective device that helps counter the nefarious attempts by those global time bandits to rob us of our leisure hours. My own version

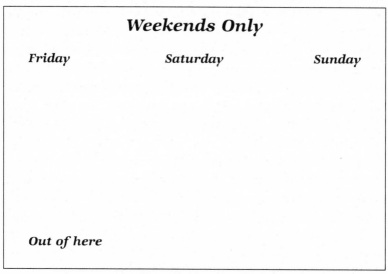

Mock-up WOC: *Schedule fun. Try some items from your Joy List.*

of the WOC is a thin magnetic wipe-off sheet that ad-heres to the refrigerator—or any other metallic sur-face—and can be reused, month after month, to plan to do anything or nothing on whichever days your "weekend" may fall.

It also includes one space for phone numbers of friends, travel agents, video rental stores, pizza deliv-ery, and so on, as well as a space for writing my new Joy List categories. Many clients provide it as a sort of touchstone to carry away from seminar presentations, and it has proven to be a favorite tool for thousands of time-warped weenies like myself.

A Humaerobic Howl for Joy

A variety of people contributed to teaching me this last exercise. But my favorite variation came from my first partner in this work, Christian Hageseth III,

M.D. a psychiatrist who, in *A Laughing Place*, explores the value of humor in coping with adversity.

It seems that Hageseth was aware of a term used by sex therapists—*erolalia*—meaning the sound of love. Supposedly, many married couples experience diminished sexual excitement because they quit making noise during lovemaking (as in, "Shhhh, you'll wake up the children").

According to the theory, when people stop expressing vocally how good their partner makes them feel, they evidently experience diminished physical sensation. Some sex therapists believe that by making loud noises, groans, whoops, and shrieks during lovemaking, people can resensitize themselves and begin to derive more physical pleasure from the act. (The act? Why do people refer to sexual intercourse as "the act"? Are you acting? Who's acting? Heaven knows, I'm not acting!)

Adapting the idea of *erolalia* to humor, Hageseth coined the term, *gelastolalia,* or the sound of laughter. The idea was that if people felt comfortable making vocal expressions of happiness, they could fully experience the deepest satisfaction of joy and good humor.

The exercise Hageseth and I devised to take advantage of this theory is called the Howl for Joy, and it's the perfect stress reliever when you're stalled in a traffic jam.

STEP 1: Start by sitting in a relaxed position.

STEP 2: Take a few deep, quieting breaths, and close your eyes.

STEP 3: Imagine something that makes you feel REALLY good. That thought might be of a person, place, or activity that brings a smile to your spirit.

I often think of my Grandmother MacDonald. This is the woman who told me: "Be careful, Butchie, when you lie it makes you smell bad, you know." The woman died more than thirty years ago, but she still makes me smile.

For you, it might be a place where you once vacationed, or hope to visit someday. It might be an activity like dancing, or fishing, or boccie ball; it might be a person; it might be a dream, a hope, a fantasy. For just a few moments, mentally focus on whatever it is that warms your spirit and brings a smile to your face.

STEP 4: Once the image is clear in your mind, gently tilt your head back a little bit, just to open the throat. Take a deep breath, and let out a howl for joy—a sound that lets you know how much that thought, picture, or image makes you feel. *AROOOOOOOOOOOOOOOOW*!

(I admit, this is getting close to stupid, and it scares some people. This is an advanced exercise, and you might want to wait a week or two before trying it.)

I often use this Humaerobic in traffic jams. There I am, stuck in a tangle of machines and madness, going nowhere, wondering why God doesn't seem to know that the Center of the Universe is late for his plane, and my gut begins to grumble. Maybe I pound the dashboard, or honk the horn, as if this magical sound will combine with the other horns and dissolve the three thousand cars in front of me. At those moments, a small voice says: "Maybe you should practice what you preach." (Actually, my wife doesn't have a small voice.)

I roll down the window, close my eyes, take a deep breath and focus on the fly-fishing trip I dream of making to New Zealand: I hook a twenty-pound brown trout on two-pound-test line with a one-ounce Orvis rod. I see the fish clearing water as it leaps toward the sun. I see myself play the trout with superb delicacy and tact. I envision the flashing, dappled red, gold, and brown of its scales as, after a thirty-minute battle, it rolls over in front of me, floating and gasping near the surface of the water. I reach down, remove the hook from its mouth, and gently guide it back toward its deep lake home to grow wiser and more wary. Then I let my head tip back slightly and I let out a howl for joy that can be heard, I think, for miles.

I grin, I laugh, I howl again. It's a wonderful exercise. I remember that I'm not just a commuter in a traffic jam. I'm not just a businessman late for a plane. I'm an ace fly-fisherman in pursuit of the mysteries of gnats and gently gurgling riffles along the rivers of heaven.

This is a fun exercise to do while bathing in the morning. It will create interesting questions at the breakfast table. Who knows, maybe the next time you snuggle up next to the love of your life, a good mutual howl will lead you to new heights of joy! That's also worth a try.

Why not Howl for Joy right now—with some consideration for your surroundings, of course—before going on to Chapter 7? So often, we let our anger out by shouting or yelling and shrieking. But how often do we allow ourselves to express how good life can make us feel for no reason other than the sheer joy of doing so? Not often enough, I think. In truth, not many people have ever howled for joy; at least, not when they were sober. Try it . You'll like it.

*Your mind is your predicament. It wants to
be free of change, free of pain, free of the
obligations of life and death. But Change is
a law, and no amount of pretending will
alter that reality.*

—*Dan Millman,* Way of the
Peaceful Warrior

7. Humor: An Antidote for Terminal Professionalism

DO you remember that mom in Texas who was convicted of trying to hire a hit man? The jury found that she had indeed offered a contract for rubbing out another mom whose daughter was competing with her own daughter for a spot on the cheerleading squad.

I have nothing against dedication to your job, whether it's raising children, directing a multinational corporation, attending college, or selling Tupperware. What does disturb me, though, is when people lose all perspective, and that loss is often attached to the prevalent idea that silliness precludes seriousness, or that humor is unprofessional.

Terminal Professionalism (TP) is an odd disease; some people actually seem to be proud that they have it. They'll walk right up to you and say, "Now, pay attention; I'm dead serious!" My response to this command is usually, "Then lie down, for heaven's sake. I'll get a shovel." There is a great deal of wisdom and self-fulfilling prophecy in the expression, *dead serious,* which lies at the heart of a modern, TP epidemic.

After a decade studying and consulting with companies throughout the world, I've become convinced that in a global economy characterized by ever-accelerating change, the failure to nourish and encourage lightness in the workplace not only undermines productivity, creativity, adaptability, and morale—it literally *drives people crazy!*

Nice Words, Scary Stuff

Throughout the eighties, many of my corporate clients were undergoing mergers, takeovers, buyouts, and downsizing. (*Downsizing* is one of my favorite euphemisms. Do they mean that they're planning to fire everyone under five-foot-five?) Toward the middle of the decade I was hired to help a major manufacturing company during its defense against an unfriendly takeover. As management knew, when layoffs are poorly handled, employee sabotage and survivor guilt frequently cost a company more than it saves. I, along with an army of other consultants, had been hired to support the people who were being laid off as well as those who were to stay on.

In the first three weeks I presented seminars to several thousand employees in two states. After intensive contact with so many people in horrible circumstances, my own sense of humor needed a boost. I got a boost, all right, but it nearly scared me to death. Following a four-hour presentation to a group of company vice presidents and managers, I was approached by a man I'll call Gene. He was a huge fellow who looked as though he had been born to live in flannel shirts and cog-boots rather than the suit and wing-tips he had on. When we shook hands, his enormous, calloused paw enveloped my much-smaller hand.

He introduced himself and said, "Do you think we could talk for a few minutes? In private?"

"No problem," I told him.

Not far away was a small conference room. I followed him inside and waited for him to start talking. Gene placed his briefcase on the table, clicked open the brass locks and lifted the top. Nestled among neat sheaves of papers was a nine-millimeter pistol with a walnut grip. I looked from the gun, to Gene, then back to the gun. The weapon's well-oiled, blue-black barrel gleamed in the fluorescent light. He laughed, and I realized that I'd heard that laugh before . . . it was the laugh of Colonel Jack D. Ripper in *Dr. Strangelove*.

Uh, oh . . .

In that moment, I realized that Gene just might be off his rocker. I knew I ought to grab the gun, or run out of the room . . . or something!

But even as I considered these options, Gene reached for the weapon. For some reason, the words, "*Oh, come on. The workshop wasn't that bad, was it?*" struck me as appropriate, but I managed to keep my mouth shut.

Gene ejected a full clip of ammo and put the gun back in the briefcase. He closed the lid, snapped the locks shut.

Then he took me by the wrist, and gently placed the clip in my palm. "Here. I want you to have this," he said. "You may not be the most brilliant speaker I've ever heard, but you said some important things this morning. Things I'd forgotten."

I don't recall every particular of every conversation, but I do remember the outline of what Gene told me that afternoon. After two decades with the company, he had been promoted to vice president. Over the next ten years he had built his department into a thriving showpiece. Then came the unfriendly take- over attempt. Gene understood that, to survive, his employer would be forced to pursue a scorched- earth policy of radical layoffs, subsidiary selloffs, and product elimination. During one hellish three-month period, Gene had been charged personally with fir- ing nearly two hundred of the men and women who worked for him.

Regardless of the company's generous benefit ex- tensions and outplacement and counseling programs, the procedure took a severe toll on Gene's mental and physical health.

"Weeks at a time," he said, "I spent nights in my office, sleeping on the couch so that I could work later and start earlier. I got a gut full of ulcers for the first time in my life. I couldn't eat right. I lost weight. My family didn't understand. Finally, my wife took our daughter and moved in with her parents. She just couldn't stand living with me any more. I had turned into a zombie."

After Gene had reduced his once-thriving depart- ment to a memory, he was told that he too was getting the axe.

"It never crossed my mind that I'd be fired, even after my department was eliminated," he told me. "I was sure that after thirty years, they'd find a place for me in the new organization. I began to think that the only reason they'd kept me on was to handle the dis- mantling. If they'd brought someone else in to fire ev- eryone, they'd have had a war on their hands."

Shortly after the company gave him notice, Gene started to keep the gun in his briefcase. At first, the idea of killing himself frightened him, but the longer he carried the gun, the more numb he felt about the prospect.

"When you talked about Terminal Professionalism today, I heard you. When you said something about taking yourself lightly and your job seriously, I realized what was happening. I didn't feel like a person any more. I had *become* my job. I didn't really want to kill myself. I wanted to kill my job."

He patted me on the shoulder with his big paw. "Maybe I'll just put a bullet in my desk and go fishing. But first, I'm going to talk to my wife and daughter. Whatever they want, I'm going to try to give it to them. Thanks, C.W. Thanks a lot."

When you can't distinguish between the human being you are and your career or your children or any such compelling force in your life, you're in a vulnerable position. When your plans come under threat or veer wildly away from your original conception, which they have a surprising way of doing, you go berserk. The usual response is to throw more time, money, or effort at the problem in the belief that you can out-work, outrun, or outlast it. Sometimes the approach works, but often the price of the effort exceeds the return.

Really Dead Serious

The Japanese have a word for the ultimate TP— *karoshi*—which means, literally, death from overwork. Medical authority Tetsunojo Uehata came up with it about ten years ago. Specifically, Uehata said, *Karoshi* is a "condition in which psychologically unsound work processes are allowed to continue in a way that disrupts the worker's normal work and life rhythms, leading to a buildup of fatigue in the body and a chronic condition of overwork accompanied by a worsening of pre-existent high blood pressure and a hardening of the arteries and finally resulting in a fatal breakdown."

We have more in common with the Japanese than we thought.

A survey released in 1991 by Nippon Kayaku Company found that currently, nine out of ten "businessmen and working women" suffer chronic fatigue; and a third of those workers blame their fatigue on overwork. One in four Japanese workers say they fear succumbing to *karoshi.*

What scares them so much?

According to the *Wall Street Journal,* in 1990, Japanese workers spent 12 hours a day working and commuting, which is about 2.5 hours more per day than their counterparts in four Western nations. In Japan a much-touted 1988 government campaign to reduce working hours to less than 2,000 within two years became a national joke when, one year later, the average Japanese put in more time on the job than before the campaign began.

Few Japanese take their entire vacations, and six-day work weeks remain the norm. Although banks complied with new government requirements to close on Saturdays, working hours increased Monday through Friday to compensate the institutions for lost time. (I don't think they quite got the idea.)

There's a "health" drink called Regain that's popular among Japanese workers. It contains caffeine, nicotine, and vitamin C. The television ad features an ambitious salary-man asking, "Can you fight twenty-four hours a day?" Apparently so if one slugs down enough Regain.

In 1987, the press blamed *karoshi* when the active presidents of ten major Japanese companies died of stress-related illness in one eight-month period.

The men died, according to one Japanese physician, because companies behave like the Japanese Army in World War II. "When one corporate officer dies," he said, "companies bring in another and another until the hill is finally won from the enemy. These businessmen are really being killed in action for the glory of the company."

They operate as they always have, but in today's changing business environment, overwork does not bring the same rewards that it did in the 1960s, and so the men push even harder.

And most Japanese companies have no special plans to solve the increasing problem of stress-related illness and death. Merit pay is still given for overwork. Peer pressure in the workplace continues to promote working long hours. A professor of economics at Konan University in Japan explained that workers "set job targets with company managers and then feel obligated to fulfill them, no matter how many hours it takes." A line from a Japanese folk tune recites the work week: "Getsu, Getsu, Ka, Sui, Moku, Kin, Kin," which translated means, "Monday, Monday, Tuesday, Wednesday, Thursday, Friday, Friday."

Can't Handle Job Stress? So, Sue Me! (Hey, I Was Just Kidding)

In 1988, a group of Japanese doctors and lawyers established the first *karoshi* telephone hotline. To date, the hotline has received reports on nearly 2,000 cases of alleged death from overwork, and suddenly, the Japanese Labor Ministry seems to have noticed the problem.

A March 1991 story in *World Press Review* reported that the widow of a Mitsui & Company employee had filed Japan's first worker-compensation claim, contending that her husband's employer had caused his death from overwork. "Jun Ishii, 47, died of acute heart failure on July 15—the last day he was assigned to guide four Soviet visitors to factory sites in Japan's Aichi Prefecture," the magazine stated. "In the 10 months prior to Ishii's death, Mitsui had dispatched him to Moscow 10 times, for a total of 103 days."

So far, Mitsui has paid Ishii's widow $225,000, awarded her an extended retirement allowance, and is assisting her in applying for workers' compensation.

Stress, American Style

In this country, too, the number of stress-related claims for damages is growing monthly. Psychologist Kenneth Pelletier says that in California alone, between 1982 and 1986, stress-related disability claims by state employees increased 434 percent. The *Wall Street Journal* reported in May 1991 that United States stress-related disability cases have doubled in the past decade and now cost the employer an average of $73,270 each.

But beyond these dire statistics, a survey commissioned by Northwestern National Life Insurance tells me that:

- Thirty-four percent of United States workers said they had considered quitting their jobs in 1990 because of excessive stress.

- Fourteen percent reported that they did quit their jobs because of excessive stress.
- One third of the workers said they believed job stress would lead them to "burn out" soon.
- Forty-six percent of workers described their jobs as highly stressful, twice as many as in 1985.

Are Loyal Employees an Endangered Species?

As most Terminally Professional managers see it, there's way too much whimpering about employee stress and too little hard work in America today. *"Stress! Stress?"* they scream. "When U.S. business is being pummeled by those workaholic Japanese, *of course* there's stress. We need more work ethic, not less," they say. "What we need is employees with good old-fashioned loyalty and old-fashioned team spirit . . . "

Eroding work ethic? Declining loyalty?

Come on. In the "good old days," people bought into the work ethic and were loyal to their employers, expecting a *clearly perceived return.* They had every reason to believe that if they gave their best to XYZ Company, and the company was successful, they would be rewarded with job security, promotions, and more money. Thus, their remarkable "loyalty."

Today's workers are cynical about the rewards of loyalty for good reason. Consider these statistics from *Business Week:* During 1985 and 1986, 600,000 jobs were eliminated because of cutbacks and restructuring. In 1989, 160,000 jobs in manufacturing were wiped out. And in the twelve months ended June 30, 1991, the American Management Association (AMA) reported that corporate downsizing had reached a

record high, with 56 percent of 910 companies sur-
veyed reporting job cuts. No wonder people suspect
that "going the extra mile" may get them an all-
expenses-paid trip to Disneyland, or, it may just earn
them a nice fat pink slip during a surprise takeover or
cost-cutting campaign.

And financial rewards? In fact, says Jack Gordon,
editor of *Training* magazine, "The gap between executive salaries and average worker salaries in the United
States has been widening since 1979—and the rift is
accelerating."

Gordon adds, "The rationale of paying millions of
dollars to a top executive is no secret. It's explained
right out loud: If we don't give him spectacular sums
of money, a rival company will lure him away."

"Curiously," Gordon observes, "when talk turns to
the fickleness of today's worker, nobody mentions the
obvious corollary: The chief is no more loyal to this
organization than anyone else."

In this climate, I ask, how can management expect
loyalty when it cannot, in honesty, promise job security in exchange? Because of the global storm of
change in business, most companies can't even promise that retirement funds will be there when employees need them.

On Your Mark, Get Set, Stop . . .

It is hard for some managers to believe that you cannot always buy employees' trust and loyalty with
dollars. But more people in today's market will, if
given the choice, choose quality of life over dollars. If
you find that hard to accept, just ask the folks at Data
General.

In 1987, when DG offered its people in Denver, Colorado, the funds to cover a move to an Eastern seaboard city, more than two thirds said no. They preferred to take their chances as free agents in the employment market rather than leave a quality of life that they considered far superior to the new environment.

The event was indicative of a radical change in American business. Even ten years earlier such balkiness would have been unheard of. Back then, when a company said, "March," the employees packed their bags, uprooted their families, and started all over again in the name of loyalty and the work ethic.

Job Insecurity

Sad but true, job security was a polite hiccup in the history of commerce. At present, average college graduates of the nineties will experience at least three or four major career changes in their working life. Although it would be satisfying to blame someone or something for this painful turn of events, decaying job security can no more be attributed to a fading work ethic or foreign competition than the breakdown of the family can be blamed on rock and roll. Both phenomena have roots in global changes in commerce, politics, technology, and demographics.

Global interdependence on raw materials and financial and agricultural resources means that job security, as it has been known in the past, can't continue. Competition is increasingly ferocious and complex; niche marketing is gobbling up many profitable little corners that once sustained megacompanies. Jobs that held solid for hundreds of years are being replaced by automation and the proliferating information and service businesses.

United States business cannot successfully compete in a global environment that pulses with change when it continues to ask that people dredge up trust and productivity from an empty well. Instead, business must begin to:

- Supplant simpleminded toughness, isolationism, and xenophobia with the more useful skills of *umor*—fluidity and adaptability.

- Find a way to nourish satisfaction, joy, pride, and fun for people on and off the job.

- Discover an acceptable, healthy alternative to Terminal Professionalism and the faded dream of job security.

Nothing from Nothing Leaves Less Than Nothing

If only a few companies valued a self-destructive work ethic, the problems caused by Terminal Professionalism would be manageable. The frightening truth is that most organizations—from local civic groups to the Fortune 100—value people who are willing to work themselves nearly to death. Consider this wisdom from *Fortune* magazine in October 1990: "Business is cracking the whip," writes Thomas A. Stewart. "A looming labor shortage, global and domestic competition, and the emphasis on speeding up work and getting costs down have made many corporations lean and mean—make that *really mean.*"

Here, as in Japan, stress has become the new red badge of courage among many hardworking, ambitious Americans—or, at least, management tends to reward those who see it that way. How sick can you get, and keep coming to work—now, **that's** professional! How 'bout that Henderson guy, eh? Massive heart attack and triple bypass surgery last night, but, he's hooked up to his IV at his desk and is dictating letters. What a pro.

The most common sideline cheer for Terminal Pros in the United States is the familiar, *Let's give it 110 percent*!

Pardon me?

You don't have to be a mathematical wizard to answer this question: If you give me 110 percent for ten days in a row, what are you left with?

(Interlude music while contestant ponders the answer.)

That's correct; if you give me 110 percent for ten days in a row, you end up 100 percent in the hole! You are one less of you than you were before you started. How many times can you deplete yourself by 100 percent and still be productive? I suppose it varies from person to person, but I begin to be substantially less productive when I give away energy that I don't really have.

I know that at times extra effort is required to accomplish a goal. My wife Roma and I have both given some projects—this book, for instance—a 200 percent effort for a specific period. When the job's finished, though, she and I will get the payoff (unlike the average United States worker). Furthermore, I follow these work jags lying in my hammock like a zucchini ripening in the sun. Roma rides a horse into the mountains, walks for hours along the beach, or rents a cartload of horror movies.

If you are *not* self-employed, however, the workplace—especially when business suffers—is rarely so considerate. Gabriella Stern wrote in the *Wall Street Journal,* "Some of the current urgency reflects pressures on chief executives themselves, who face increased scrutiny from stockholders and directors for improved results because of the weak economy."

Many of the driving human forces behind business are convinced that it's fine to put on the pressure and squeeze a few more productivity points out of a department, manager, or CEO. After all, the reasoning goes, that's what we pay 'em for, right?

If that is what a company is paying people for, it does so at the risk of self-annihilation.

The end result of Terminal Professionalism is that a company burns out its best people at just about the time their experience might be of real value, or it leaves them walking around with resentment so deep they are constantly sabotaging projects.

As I mentioned earlier, *when the going gets tough, the tough get going* approach can backfire. Quite frequently, throwing more time, money, and energy at problems merely exhausts people. Those approaches may have worked when things got tough once a quarter. Back *then,* you had time to rest between bouts of intense activity. These periods of respite allowed you to savor success and draw meaningful conclusions from your failures.

Now, the ascending rate of change has made things tough every day. We're having to adapt more often, with less preparation, on more issues, than at any other time in history. Giving 110 percent in such a world inevitably leads us to lose our creative edge, grow cynical more quickly, burn out faster, and spend more time in pouting than producing.

If you're anything like I am you'll be tempted to try all the following techniques at once. I advise against fanaticism. An obsessive approach to lightening up will only increase your stress.

Perhaps, however, you are certain that cultivating a lighter attitude can't work for you.

Maybe you're right.

But, you won't know until you try working happier instead of working harder. Remember, what you're after here is to avoid the tendency to become hard, brittle, and easily broken. The intention is to explore *umor*, fluidity, adaptability, and progress in the face of challenge, crisis, and change.

For you as an individual, the payoff can be worth the effort. You can be professional, hardworking, intelligent, successful, AND have a good time that includes humor, health, family, and friends.

Draw the Line!

We hear it all the time: "Leave your work at the office."

"Thanks," I want to say to such Pollyannas, "I never thought of that. How very helpful. But, why don't I just leave *you* at the office?"

In fact, learning to leave your work at the office is difficult, especially if, as a house spouse, your home *is* your office. Yes, difficult, but essential if you hope to avoid the corruption of TP.

The first thing I had to learn to do was *Draw the Line*—create a ritual celebrating the end of work and the beginning of the rest of my life. It wasn't just a matter of walking out of the office, getting in the car, and driving home. No matter how hard most of us try, work, like a passel of nagging gremlins, has a way of hiding in our briefcases and following us home. There has to be a ritual, a deliberate act of severance, a celebration of our reentry into the rest of life. Otherwise, the gremlins nibble at us all afternoon and into the evening. They drain us of strength that we need for vital relationships with our families and friends. Sometimes the nasty creatures gnaw at our dreams and leave us more tired than refreshed when we awaken.

Desk Training: A favorite Draw-the-Line technique was a gift from the vice president of a large midwestern industrial plant. Ralph takes the last five or ten minutes of each work day to list all the unfinished tasks that he knows will follow him home and make his life miserable. He then puts the list in a special desk drawer, locks it, and hangs the key on the wall. As he backs out of the office, he points at the desk and says firmly, "Stay!"

Stupid?

No, it's silly. (Remember? Silly used to be considered a blessing.) It's an act of *umor* that allows him to:

1. Make fun of his fears.
2. Define the difference between himself and his work.
3. Affirm his right to a sense of joy in being alive— the third humor skill—by acting out his right to leave his work at work.

Nose Job: A group of businesswomen I know assembled a slightly more expensive Draw-the-Line ritual— it cost them about a buck—when they decided to purchase a batch of foam-rubber clown noses, one for each of them. They left the noses in the glove boxes of their cars and, when they headed out on the traffic-jammed road trip home, they put the noses on.

"The sight of my reflection in the rear-view mirror makes it impossible for me to think of myself as having any right to think about work. And the looks I get from other drivers range from disgust to hysteria," said one woman, "My favorite trick is to stop on the way home and do a bit of shopping while wearing my red clown nose. The funny thing is, very rarely does anyone mention it! It's as though, if I'm having a good time in a public place, there must be something wrong with me."

Another woman told me about using the clown nose to help her husband Draw the Line. One night when she knew he would have to work late, Jean dressed in sexy lingerie and her clown nose and waited for him in bed. That ploy led to one of the silliest, sexiest nights of their marriage. (Her follow-up story of how, the next night, her husband came to bed wearing his own clown nose in a very unusual place will have to wait for the *Humor and Marriage* book.)

A Bare Necessity: My own Draw-the-Line exercise may be of value to other bald people. I bought a wig that I keep on the hat rack in my office. At the end of the day, I pop it on and slip out the door. Why does it work? Well, it's a curly, longish, strawberry-blond number—nothing subtle about it. And, much as my job may want to follow me home, the job is waiting for a bald guy to leave. My job doesn't recognize me in that hairpiece! The wig is a simple, effective way to celebrate the end of my work day and the beginning of the rest of my life.

Draw-the-Line exercises are legion among my clients. They may be simple, but they do serve an important purpose. People disconnect from Terminal Professionalism while consciously taking control of their free time and energy. The most common benefit is that people who Draw the Line begin to find that this act of respect and reverence for their own relaxation and pleasure strengthens their job performance. Why? Because rest and pleasure allow people to renew themselves. Because even though we work, even though we have problems, people still have to be people. By Drawing the Line they are able to work with far less tension and hostility, in a more creative and positive frame of mind.

Going Batty: Secret Silliness

Perhaps Terminal Professionalism is so highly valued in your work environment that you can't imagine how to incorporate humor skills without losing your job. Maybe your boss is convinced that if you haven't had an ulcer by age twenty-nine, a heart attack by age thirty-seven, and a long separation or a divorce by age forty, you are not serious enough about your career.

You still have choices.

First, you can find another job. But take warning. It is perfectly possible to take Terminal Professionalism with you when you clean out your office. Some of the most driven, dead-serious people I know are entrepreneurs working in home offices.

If switching jobs or self-employment is not practical, you have a second choice. Some practitioners have applied this technique under various code names: the Goofiness Guild, the Unprofessional Underground, or, as a group of particularly joyful Catholic nuns named it—the Sisters of Secret Silliness.

The purpose of such groups is to help people in the Terminally Professional workplace avoid burnout, while also avoiding dismissal or reprimand. The techniques used by Silly Societies are usually simple but effective in relieving stress, affirming one's right to life, laughter, and looseness, at the same time bonding coworkers. One of my favorite examples is a secret Wall Street society called the UU.

It's What's Underneath That Counts

A group of young stockbrokers who work for a particularly TP Wall Street firm have taken to wearing Mickey Mouse underwear to work every Friday. They call themselves the UU—underwear underground.

"Nobody knows but the UU members," one young woman told me. "We have a secret handshake and a specific way of waving to each other, which identifies and bonds us in our resistance to becoming Terminally Professional."

Another UU member told me, "If the management knew why we were so productive and happy at work, I'm sure they'd be appalled, but our motto is: *What They Don't Know Won't Hurt Us.*"

Help for the Terminally Professional Employer

Employers ought to be begging to help people find the most enjoyable, fulfilling, and creative way of doing their jobs. Business needs to discover the true value of its enterprises. Instead of focusing on profit as a sole motive, it must allow profit to become a by-product of superb service and quality. Sure, companies couldn't exist without profits, but face it: *overall* corporate profit hardly provides the average employee with thrills and chills. (Someone told me that thinking of profit as by-product rather than motive sounded like a communist conspiracy. But that's a weak argument these days because, along with clean air and drinkable water, we are beginning to run out of communists.)

Aiming to provide superb service and high quality, and having a sense of performing a valuable service, however, *can* inspire company-wide enthusiasm and creativity. But quality and innovation are not the products of a constantly driven, Terminally Professional work force. The truth is that humor in the work environment (in combination with management's guidance and support, and having the freedom to explore ideas) leads employees to become better, creative problem solvers.

Research shows that "putting people in a good mood by telling them jokes makes them think through problems with more ingenuity," writes Daniel Goleman in *The New York Times*. "Casual joking at work may thus improve people's effectiveness in their tasks."

Alice M. Isen, a psychologist at the University of Maryland in Baltimore, remarks that, "Any joke that makes you feel good is likely to help you think more broadly and creatively." Innovation, says Isen, is facilitated by the elation people experience after hearing a "good joke."

To cultivate an energetic and creative work force, I begin by suggesting that you ask your employees for their best 90 percent (not 110 percent) daily. That way, over a five-day work week, they can accumulate a full 50 percent to spend in nonwork-related fun on the weekend. It makes sense that such an approach would create people who were happier (morale goes up), healthier (health-care costs go down), more productive (profits would be up), more creative (providing an edge over the competition), and loyal. (You might think twice about going elsewhere to work for more money if you knew you wouldn't have as much time to enjoy it.)

Quit Promoting Workaholism

Don't cultivate workaholism and don't hire workaholics. (Ouch, I know that one hurts.)

Naturally enough, in its zeal to cut overhead and improve efficiency, management is attracted to people who can't or won't stop working. (Often those people are put in charge of less-driven Type Bs, to everybody's eventual dissatisfaction.) But though hiring a workaholic sounds great in theory, in practice it usually doesn't pay.

Overwork over an extended period correlates with deteriorating performance. According to psychologist Robert Rosen, *workaholics*—those sterling examples of Terminal Professionalism—rarely are more productive than less-driven individuals.

What exactly is the difference between *working hard* and *workaholism*?

Rosen says that workaholics are frequently consumed by work for the sake of being active, not for results. Other workaholics use their addiction to avoid personal problems, or as a vent for chronic anger, or to bolster shaky self-esteem.

Hard workers, Rosen explains, produce tangible results that are commensurate with the time applied. In my own observation, hard workers do take pleasure and find meaning in work, but their careers fit into a larger pattern of lives. Most significantly, hard workers can take part in leisure activities without experiencing withdrawal pain or guilt.

Are there exceptions? Is there such a thing as positive work addiction?

I've known people who seem obsessed by a desire to contribute to life through their career. Often, such people have been entrepreneurs, researchers, thinkers, whose personalities were balanced by a love of living that stretched far beyond their professional endeavors. I don't suppose they are true workaholics, but no matter how excited they are by work, *almost everyone* reaches a point of human limitation, exhaustion, and diminishing returns.

And what about the geniuses, prodigies, world and spiritual leaders who operate on a seemingly higher plane—women and men who sacrifice their personal lives because they are consumed by a desire to create great art, or to fulfill a personal vision of world healing or peace? Well, far be it from me to advise people like Mother Teresa, a woman who begins her days with prayer at 4:30 A.M., and considers her constant service to the poor as God's work, and herself as a mere "pencil in his hand."

For all of us who are less than saintly, here are some tools for bringing humor into the Terminally Professional workplace.

Work, of Course! But Let It Be Fun

Keeping customers happy is such an important part of a flight attendant's job that Southwest Airlines has made humor part of the job description. The airline recruits people with "a strong sense of humor," who, along with serving well, smiling, and communicating well, "have been known to recite the safety regulations in rap, bring out a guitar and sing and wear costumes on Halloween flights," according to the *Wall Street Journal.* A standard interview question asks job candidates to describe their most embarrassing moment and how they got out of it with humor.

What do the customers think of the happy attendants? Do they long for increased gravity in the air? To find out, in April 1991, Southwest began having its frequent fliers interview flight-attendant candidates, and "almost across the board," said the *Wall Street Journal,* the frequent fliers' choices were identical to the airline's.

Along with pleasing the customers, the airline's emphasis on fun apparently contributes to healthy company morale. Southwest's 9,000 employees are known for their loyalty and hard work. When oil prices jumped in autumn 1990, "employees bought the airline $135,000 worth of jet fuel through payroll deductions." As for the company's bottom line, at the end of 1990, Southwest was the only major American airline to report an operating and net profit. Other businesses too have found a light heart good for business.

- At *New Age* magazine, the staff lightens up daily with a whiffle-ball game at lunch, deadline or no deadline.

- One of our clients, the prestigious and profitable Nationwide Broadcasting, Inc., has seen executives show up for boardroom meetings in clown noses or fright masks. (President Steve Berger insists that he is *not* wearing a mask.)

- At one Hewlett-Packard plant where we had offered several humor trainings, employees created a Lighten-Up Library, similar to those which have been established in hundreds of hospitals around the world. The group began by decorating a small room with a wild and vivid paint job. "The idea," said a participant, "was to use all the primary colors like on kids' blocks; you know, lime-green, carrot-orange, apple-red; those colors reminded everyone of childhood."

The room was stocked with magazines, books, posters, and video and audio programs that people felt were either funny or uplifting. A corkboard sheet was put up so that participants could display their favorite cartoons and pictures of themselves and their families doing goofy things. The room was used for brown-bag lunches, upbeat conversations, and minivacation breaks.

That management approved of and even took part in decorating the room boosted everyone's spirits.

Let People Value Family and Friends (They Will Anyway)

Perhaps it is a sign of mental health that in a survey conducted by International Research Associates and the Roper Organization, Americans ranked their occupations eighth in importance among ten things affecting their lives. Here is the list:

1. Children's education.
2. Family life.
3. Health.
4. Quality of life.

5. Friends, relatives.
6. Love life.
7. Income, standard of living.
8. Occupation.
9. Leisure activities.
10. Current political situation.

Although *Incentive* magazine referred to that survey as a testimonial to the decline of the American work ethic (the Japanese listed their occupations as second in importance; and for the Europeans, occupation came fourth), I feel compelled to ask all managers whether they *really* believe employees *should* value their jobs more than or even as much as they value their families, friends, and health.

I believe that if management can bring the best interests of business into line with workers' best interests, employees will have more reason to take pride in workmanship and loyalty to company. True, companies can no longer guarantee job security, but they can contribute to employees' health and well-being rather than detract from it if they will support a campaign to stamp out Terminal Professionalism before it stamps them out.

The joy of joys is the person of light but unmalicious humor.

—*Emily Post*, **Etiquette: The Blue Book of Social Usage**

8. Can't You Take a Joke? Etiquette for the Humor Impaired

I WAS recently dining with a group of managers who had just attended one of my presentations and I cringed when one of the men at our table began to tell a joke that was obviously going to put women down.

"You know how to put a twinkle in a woman's eye?" he asked.

"No, and I'm not sure I want to," I said lightly, hoping to deflect the punch line. It didn't work.

"Why, just shine a flashlight in her ear," he said. To my astonishment, everyone at the table laughed, including the women—though not quite as heartily.

Then one of the women said cheerfully to the joker, "Knowing you, Bud, I'm afraid that's the only way you could put a twinkle in a woman's eye."

Again, everyone laughed loudly. The guy who had started it all laughed loudest. As it turned out, in that group of managers the men and women had openly agreed that, rather than hide their tensions about working together, they would let the sexist jokes roll, but everyone would have the right to take shots at everyone else.

Any member of the group who was hurt or offended by someone's jibes said so, and the perpetrator who didn't let up lost all humor rights and had to take shots from everyone, without retaliating, for a week. Although this solution to coping with sexist humor in the workplace has shortcomings, it is certainly an improvement over less-open methods I've seen. The truth is that although humor can build trust, it has equal power to destroy it.

As Freud suggests, humor *does* allow us to be malicious while maintaining some modicum of dignity. But when that meanness is focused on us, we generally don't feel dignified. When comedy becomes a weapon, the enemy is confused. Just like ridicule directed at a child, an attack that ends with, "What's the matter, can't you take a joke?" or, "You have no sense of humor!" denies the target any chance for defense or a response that might relieve tension, resentment, and anger. Humor as a hammer is so common, its positive and negative values are so confounding, that many of us choose to abandon it altogether. It is essential to establish some rules for healthy humor if you are to avoid abusing yourself and others.

Looking for Laughs in All the Wrong Places

Emily Post wrote in the 1940s that what the would-be humorist says is unimportant. "It is the twist he gives to it, and the intonation, the personality he puts into his quip or retort or observation that delights his hearers, and to his case the ordinary rules do not apply." In other words, successful humorists have an art and a knack that may serve them well, but the attempt may flop or cause damage when imitated by others.

As a victim of childhood teasing, I can guarantee that even though ridicule and other forms of abusive humor may get you a laugh, they have *no* socially redeeming value unless you are:

1. Paying to observe them at the local comedy club. (If abusive humor makes you laugh, I understand, because, as someone recently told me, "You can't always be young, but you *can* stay immature forever.")

2. Being paid to perform; that is, you are a comic known and loved for insult humor.

3. Absolutely certain that the object of abuse is amused; and how can you *really* be sure? Safe humor (like safe sex) is 100 percent safe only when you abstain or stick to yourself as the subject. If you're fat and you want to make fat jokes, great. If you're Polish and you want to make Polish jokes, fine. Plenty of comics have gotten rich this way.

4. Exchanging oral abuse with other consenting adults as part of an accepted social ritual with defined boundaries. Such insults usually are absurd exaggerations rather than personal cuts.

Red Cape of Courage

Like everyone except Orphan Annie, my sense of humor was shaped by my family. Growing up in an unstable family in which everyone's behavior seemed to orbit my father's alcoholism, I remember feeling as if I were a tiny matador in a ring where the bull sometimes went berserk; it was my job to distract and thereby prevent him from doing too much damage. I learned quickly that he who creates comic diversion avoids a beating—or, at least, diverts people enough to make the shouting stop. As I did so, jokes and clowning around became my red cape of self-defense.

But another mediating factor influenced my attitude toward humor: the same father who often created havoc and despair in the household was at times one of the funniest guys in town. People loved Dad for his sense of humor. Here was a man who, at any gathering, could evoke smiles, happiness, and laughter with his wit and playfulness. Even drunk, he was often (but not always) funnier than he was scary. The Dr. Jekyll and Mr. Hyde quality of his alcoholic personality was enormously confusing, as it is for millions of kids who grow up in similar environments, and left me with mixed emotions about all kinds of mirth.

It was teasing, however, that really warped my sense of humor. When other kids dubbed me "dog boy" because of my hairy, early entry into puberty, or tormented me for being too skinny or too poor, my low self-regard sank lower, and my ambivalence toward jokes and jokers intensified.

In the summer of my tenth year, after my parents divorced, I was sent to live on my aunt and uncle's farm. Marge and Ed, themselves childless, often acted as temporary foster parents, taking in wards of the court. Roy was fifteen when he joined us. Smooth and street-wise, he became the terror of my childhood. Around my aunt and uncle, he was the kind of kid adults refer to as "a decent boy who gets rambunctious at times." Around other kids he was Freddie Kruger with a "sense of humor." It was Roy who tied firecrackers to the dog's tail and laughed gleefully as the small terrier ran yelping across the fields.

I don't think the other kids wanted to play when

Roy came up with the arrow game, but he made it an offer they couldn't refuse.

I was tied to a stack of haybales and Roy charged the others twenty-five cents to shoot arrows at me. The object of the game was to get as close to me as possible without hitting me. If they hit me, or missed by more than three feet, they had to come up with another two bits. After three rounds, the winner would get half the money and Roy the rest. But he was not completely vicious. Roy filed the target points to a flat, blunt end that, when they struck me, were intended to bruise rather than impale—unless of course they took out an eye. As I said, however, Roy wasn't all mean. He announced a fifty-cent fine for anyone whose arrow struck me above the shoulders.

They played the arrow game only once. The other kids simply stopped coming around until a county official discovered that Roy had tried to pawn my aunt's silverware in town, and the boy's stay was cut short. Once, however, was enough to teach me yet again that the world was a dangerous place.

Years later I would be able to look back and see a peculiar kind of humor in what had happened—the arrow game did, after all, prepare me well for understanding the world of business and politics—but at the time I was haunted by the sound of Roy's laughter, the whistle and thunk of those arrows lodging in the haybales, the pain magnified by terror when one of them glanced off a rib.

The Genderation Gap

Like so many other people, my sense of powerlessness, fear, anger, and distrust combined to reinforce the idea that if somebody was laughing, then someone must be getting hurt. And, in my world, it was usually men who were doing the hurting.

In recent years I have come to see that men—especially men like me—need to learn to trust and cultivate meaningful friendships with each other if they are to be free of self-doubt and self-loathing. But as a boy growing up in a family in which the women took responsibility when life got rough, it seemed to me that men were untrustworthy, uncaring, and undependable. The decent guys, like my brother-in-law George Roberts, died young. My mother, who worked most of her life to support her children, had to earn a living in an environment where divorced working women were often seen as failures, if not objects of contempt. And it had been my grandmother who nurtured me earlier, an older sister who cared for me when Mom went looking for work, and a neighbor woman I called Aunt Mae, who watched over me when Mom was gone.

In one way or another, I felt, men were untrustworthy. I have met women and men whose experience led them to exactly the opposite prejudice, but either way, such reverse sexism is a tremendous block to humor development. My gender-based perception of humor was complicated when Mom moved my sister and me from the mostly rural community we'd grown up in to the city of San Jose. It was there that my increasingly warped sense of humor got truly twisted. I added the neat trick of becoming a reverse racist as well.

Adding Insults to Injuries

Because my mother's income was minimal, we lived on the wrong side of the tracks. In fact, we lived almost *on* the tracks, in a warehouse district of the city's rapidly expanding industrial section.

I began to attend a racially mixed school (so *mixed* that whites came close to constituting a minority), where I learned a great deal about friendship, trust, and interracial difficulty. As a poor kid from what was then referred to as a *broken home*, I soon discovered what it was like to be victimized by racist humor. The white kids at school slandered me for hanging out with the blacks, Chicanos, and Asians, who were, because we lived in the same part of town, becoming my friends. In *Ethnic Families in America,* the authors comment that "feelings of belonging to a certain group of people for whatever reason, are a basic feature of the human condition." My sense of belonging was solidified a year after our arrival in San Jose when, at age twelve, I was accepted into a mostly non-white street gang. There I learned my expertise in the verbal karate of *dozens.*

Based on a "game" that has roots in Islamic, Celtic, and African cultures, dozens was probably brought to America by black slaves. Two people curse one another as creatively and colorfully as possible until one of them loses his or her temper; an opponent who gets angry and starts swinging loses. I was rarely able to come out a winner in any physical fight, but get me trading "your momma" insults and I was rarely defeated.

All these years later, I've come to understand that, in one form or another, dozens is a primary form of communicating between people who can't express softness, silliness, or play without feeling threatened. In the ghetto the game served to toughen young black men against the insults and degradation they would face later in life. But insult humor is in no way limited to African-American culture. Unless, of course, I missed something and Andrew Dice Clay is wearing a lot of makeup.

Although circumstance led me away from the gang and the ghetto a few years later, I carried traces of resentment toward whites—especially white males—for years. That reverse racism was broken in the mid-eighties. Following a workshop for a gathering of United States educators, I was approached by a wiry, sharply dressed man whose skin had that remarkable deep, purple-black sheen that seems to radiate light. He smiled. I smiled in return.

He came close, rested his hand on my shoulder, and spoke quietly. "I've been on the planet for fifty-seven years, son, and I've lived in nine countries. I've known all kinds. But, you're an odd one; you don't like white folks, son. I've had a touch of trouble with that myself, so I recognize the signs. Every derogatory reference you made today was about *The Man*. The next time you look in a mirror, pay attention; you didn't grow up to be a black saxophone player, if you know what I mean. You don't have to hate white to love color, or vice versa. Just take it all in and love it. It's hard, but anything else just makes you sicker."

Then he walked away. He was right. It hasn't been easy, but it has been worth it.

The Humor of Hate

As to how *dangerous* racist humor can be, a B'nai B'rith study shows that throughout history, public acceptance of anti-Semitic jokes has often been a prelude to Jewish persecution.

Hostility and aggression are the point of racist and sexist jokes and people derive enjoyment from a sense of triumph over the group that is being put down. The temporary sense of superiority that elicits laughter in such joking holds up only if we do not identify with the target group. A sure sign of small-minded racist or sexist joking is demonstrated if the jokers cannot appreciate the humor when it is turned back on them.

Change engenders fear. Fear breeds hatred. Hatred thrives on blame. In world history, when great changes have threatened the status quo, ignorant, overburdened, excessively pious, and plainly psychopathic individuals have used blame to wrest an illusion of order and control from the midst of chaos. Rather than accept responsibility for learning to live in a transitional environment, they blame some "enemy" who can be obliterated.

Should anyone be foolish enough to suggest that these righteous individuals lighten up for a moment, the result is apt to be resentment, even violence. The only humor they appreciate is racist and ethnic—the kind that separates them from their "enemies."

Hate movements are the visible diseases revealing any society's loss of perspective; and I pity people who are caught up in them. Because I must, I grant them their right to opinions, and to legal recourse in attempts to gain their ends. But that doesn't stop me from wishing I could spray them all with laughing gas.

Comedy's Common Claws

Recognizing that individual history will shade our understanding of positive and negative humor, some elements of laughter, joy, fun, and play affect all of us.

At the simplest physical level, smiling and laughter are motor reflexes involving "the coordinated contraction of fifteen facial muscles in a stereotyped pattern and accompanied by altered breathing." (Whew!) You can *always* get people to smile and laugh by applying electric shocks of varying intensity to the zygomatic major (the main lifting muscle of the upper lip).

You will *sometimes* get them to laugh by tickling them in the ribs, telling jokes, showing cartoons or funny movies, making funny faces, exchanging fond looks with them, and so on. People probably laugh more often because they feel good, or because their companions please them (smiling and laughter really are catching), than because somebody has told a joke. Experts point out that humor is "the only form of communication in which a stimulus on a high level of complexity produces a stereotyped, predictable response on the physiological reflex level."

Babies laugh fifteen times more often when tickled by their mothers than they do when strangers tickle them. According to *Encyclopaedia Britannica,* "The child will laugh only—and this is the crux of the matter—when it perceives tickling as a mock attack."

Children often use teasing to put down others who are different. Boys tease and belittle girls. Girls tease and belittle boys. The young joke about the old. A disturbing fact about the potent effects of racism in American culture is reflected in studies showing that at an early age white children are amused by disparagement of nonwhite victims.

Similar studies found that among three- to six-year-old children, *only whites* found it funnier to see a child of another ethnic group disparaged than one of their own. Black and Mexican-American children do not exhibit such preferences at an early age.

These studies suggest that one of the earliest lessons about comedy is that laughter is at the expense of those who are socially disadvantaged relative to oneself. They also suggest that nonwhites in our country learn to respond with disparaging humor in self-defense.

Elders in our culture are often the victims of ageist humor. Nancy Datan says in *Humor and Aging* that the use of humor in society often serves a double purpose. "First, it may reassure the young that the old are distant from themselves—an unwholesome purpose. . . . " In part, this kind of humor grows from the dread younger people have of their own aging. The effect of this kind of humor is that the *other* is by definition inferior, and the result is a form of social segregation.

Second, Datan points out, humor may serve the "outgroup or the stranger" by strengthening identity, "whether through the humor of self-disparagement or through the humor of power."

Although comedy can be used to injure and separate, it can also be used to transform anxiety to pleasure. (Consider comedian George Burns's classic line, "I'm glad to be here; but, at my age, I'm glad to be anywhere.")

Ultimately, humor can become an elder's banner of freedom (as in 101-year-old Sylvie Washington's observation, "When I was younger, I always had to pay attention to pleasing everybody but me. The best thing about being 101 is I don't give a fiddle and two farts about what anybody thinks of me any more. I'm more interested in what I think of them!'').

Family foolishness is as potentially dangerous as it is life giving. Although the complexities of family humor are too numerous for in-depth discussion in a single chapter, let alone a few paragraphs, I do want to make some suggestions. I have noticed that joking among family members takes two primary forms: one-sided, abusive humor, and interactive supportive humor.

The most unfortunate example I've seen of one-way, abusive humor in families has to do with parent-child teasing. Fathers and mothers are often uncomfortable with the emerging sexuality of their children, and siblings may experience a similar uneasiness.

The tension may find release with parents teasing daughters about boyfriends, use of makeup, the need for a bra, and so on. If, for instance, Dad starts to joke about his daughter's anatomy, makeup, or boyfriends, she might try to defend herself with a line like, "If your big belly bothered you as much as my personal life, maybe you'd lose some weight like Mom says you should!"

Dad's reply is often: "Hey, wait a minute; don't talk to me like that. What's the matter, can't you take a joke?"

To confused fathers and mothers, let me say that, no, quite frequently she *can't* take a joke. Considering that a young girl emerging into womanhood is already faced with a barrage of social expectations—physical and biological changes so intense that her emotions are in a perpetual slide between anxiety and euphoria—I think that's enough. By disallowing her to fight back, you're negating her right to feel, and you're setting up a communication pattern that may distort her interactions with men for years to come.

Parent-son teasing can be equally destructive. Although boys are, according to popular cultural stereotypes, less sensitive than girls, the truth is that their feelings can be hurt just as easily. As adolescents, they are awkward and anxious at times. They become self-conscious about their physical changes—big feet, deep voices, humiliating clumsiness. Teasing, like other forms of shaming, can, as Robert Bly points out in *Iron John,* create wounds that refuse to heal.

There are families, however, where tension, confusion, and differences are handled better. My friends, the Baribaults, seem close to ideal when it comes to handling sticky interactions. Bill and Sue are young parents, or so they appear to me. Their children—Paul, eighteen, and Marianne, thirteen—have become two of my best young friends. (We could be closer if they would let me win at Ping-Pong more often, but neither of them seems overly concerned with my delicate ego. That's good. I think that's right. But, gee, once in a while?)

One of the first things I noticed about their family was the open, two-way form of kidding, joking, and limit-setting that marks their communication.

Sue and the kids sometimes tease Dad about his obsession with *family meetings.*

"Too many Ozzie and Harriet shows when he was a child," Paul once said.

Bill's response was, "You'd rather we ran this family like the Simpsons?"

"Don't have a cow," Marianne giggled.

"I think we already do," Sue said. "I mean, act like the Simpsons. Not have a cow. Do we have a cow?"

After they'd all taken their shots, a family meeting began. What I saw in that exchange was that Bill, as the temporary leader of the discussion, gained power and respect by being amused by the razzing, rather than taking offense at it. I've seen the kids and Sue do the same thing when they called meetings to discuss issues. **They use two-way comedy—jokes intended to bond, not separate—that relieve tension instead of creating it.**

Marianne, at thirteen, is rocketing into womanhood with a potent combination of athletic ability, physical beauty, and social awareness. Bill expresses pride in her, operating in the knowledge that trust has always been the basis of their family interaction. Limits are set, but only after a discussion that includes everyone involved. Humor has always been encouraged as a way of dealing with difficult or embarrassing issues. **Theirs is a positive humor of love, limits, looseness, and letting go.**

Of Justices and Jokes

I guess that it's a healthy sign of increasing sensitivity that in 1991 the problem of sexual harassment in the workplace was finally brought into the spotlight when law professor Anita Hill accused Supreme Court nominee Judge Clarence Thomas of sexual harassment in the workplace. Yet, as I watched the televised debacle created by the Senate Judiciary Committee's mulling over of Thomas's alleged improprieties, I couldn't help thinking that this public display had become an exercise in self-defeat. True, the case *did* provide every comic in the country with enough fresh material to build a show, but on the downside, it created further tension, mistrust, and confusion in the tricky arena of female and male relations.

Since the public hearings, my clients frequently ask how to handle humor in the workplace. Should men take shots at women under any circumstances? Is it okay for anyone—male or female—to make light of the opposite sex?

Some of the people who approach me think that all this *sensitivity stuff* has gone too far, subsequently eliminating one of the few, relatively safe, tension-release valves available to male and female coworkers; others are glad that the Hill and Thomas case put everyone on notice that harassment is a serious issue.

I tend to agree with the writers of an article that appeared in the October 21, 1991 issue of *Time* magazine. "Once the ground settles under everyone's feet, perhaps the intricacies of the law will become less important, because the standards of acceptable behavior will have been forever raised." I hope that the stress endured by both Hill and Thomas serves this larger purpose.

Until men and women can work, play, laugh, cry, and hope together without benefit of court proceedings, the tools offered in this chapter can help. Some form of humor has to be maintained in our professional lives, or we'll all tighten up and snap.

Yes, mistakes will inevitably be made, feelings will be hurt, sensitivities offended, and often the jerks will prevail. But I'm convinced that most of us can grow beyond the confinements of suspicion, bigotry, and hypocrisy to find a humor that is bonding.

Learning from the Community of Comics

"If you're going to tell 'em the truth, make 'em laugh, or they'll kill you," said the late Ernie Kovacs. Don Rickles took up the challenge and perfected insult humor in the sixties and seventies. But his "insult humor" was more put-on than a put-down. You left Don's shows feeling that you had more in common with different kinds of people, rather than that you were different from or better than others. Andrew Dice Clay has taken abusive comedy to new depths in the eighties and nineties. No matter what you may think about such stuff, it probably relieves someone's tension. Certainly, some people view Clay's humor as satire, or as an acceptable bridge between prejudice and integration. (It's acceptable to *some people,* I said, but I'm not one of them.)

Whether or not you find Rickles or Clay funny, you make an agreement when you go to this kind of performance to take what is dished out—or leave. (That's why we call this America.) If you are easily offended, check the reviews before you buy a ticket. I don't know of a comic who has significantly affected public behavior, except, perhaps, Lenny Bruce. And all Lenny did was tell the truth at the wrong time.

As a rule, comics reflect the absurdity of human behavior. When they do explore new territory and social limits or needs, they usually shed light on current problems. If comics alone were capable of changing society, the world would be a much better place for the likes of Will Rogers, John Henton, Elaine Boozler, Mike Nichols and Elaine May, or Lily Tomlin.

One element in Robin Williams's comedy that has always impressed me is his ability to focus on the foibles, absurdities, and razor edges of human behavior without losing compassion. Some politicians and public figures might argue with me, but his act is devoid of abusive, personal attacks—*except when he's heckled.* And you'd better have the devil on your side if you are stupid enough to try to heckle Mr. Williams.

I saw Robin take on a huge drunken male who was shouting obscenities toward the stage. Robin stopped, fixed the man with an ominous glare, and the place went silent. Then Robin began trembling and actually appeared to froth at the mouth. (Remember, this guy was a top student at Julliard, one of the best acting schools in the world.) Then he shouted in an insane, shrieking voice, "That's enough! I can't take it any more!"

The audience was stunned. Had he really gone over the edge?

Robin leapt from the stage, tore through the audience, sat down beside that slobbering whale, and began imitating him as though they were *both* drunken jerks watching the stage. Robin pushed it. He pushed it hard. The man was totally befuddled. Robin had made him just what he had wanted to be—part of the act. But the obscene behemoth wasn't too sure he liked it. People were laughing. The heckler had had enough. Just as he appeared to be moving toward an act of physical mayhem, Robin leapt to his feet, slapped the guy on the back, and cried out to the audience, "Give this guy a big hand, he was brilliant, wasn't he?"

The audience applauded. Robin thanked the heckler for being such a big help, and returned to his place on the stage. Not another word was heard from the drunk.

Watching Robin work at stand-up comedy, you come to appreciate just how thin that edge between negative and positive humor really is, and what genius it takes to honor and make an art of it. It should also let you know that mere mortals like ourselves need to be very careful with positive and negative humor, and to forgive ourselves and others when we misuse it from ignorance or fear.

Of all the professional comics I've known, Danny Mora has the surest grasp on the art and craft of the business. His comedy workshop, the Peer Group, has operated in Los Angeles since 1976. Although Mora is a talented television actor and writer with credits going back to *Chico and the Man* and *Laverne and Shirley,* he is even better known as a trainer, coach, and friend to the most successful comics in the business. Danny's observations about comedy are among the best explanations of the difference between positive and negative humor I have come across.

Mora advises comics to approach the audience as though everyone came to have a good time. "We're a community—the challenge isn't, can I control them, or outfight them?" he says. "It's not a combat or control issue; the challenge is to find what we have in common. What can I give them that might help? When great comics succeed, they don't do it by fighting the audience. They do it by creating a community in time and space."

Dan believes that vulnerability is required too. "You have to let the audience know who you are. You have to be as open with them as you're going to ask them to be with you. You have to walk through your fear of failure by making a fool of yourself. Come on! That's your job! Celebrating the absurdity of it all. Laughing until the hurt is healed, and finding the joy in the junk yard, man . . . that's what great comedy is all about!"

"Short of that," Mora says, "if you can get the club manager to pay you more than fifty bucks for a twenty-minute set, you're a success."

Starting with Danny's conviction that communion and community are the basis of positive comedy, and drawing from my own experience, research by learned loonies, and a little help from my friends, I think it's possible to lay down some flexible guidelines for the proper use of humor.

Before you try kidding around, **know your audience.** This rule applies whether the audience is one person or a thousand. That infants respond positively to being tickled by their mothers, but fearfully to being tickled by strangers, explains more about the human experience of positive and negative humor than a mountain of psychological testing. Positive humor occurs between people who know each other. In one way or another, they have gained each other's permission to use fun, laughter, play, or jokes to affirm their relationship.

Negative humor is an attack disguised as a joke that allows the offender to avoid responsibility for his or her actions. It leaves the victim with only two apparent choices. One is to laugh, swallow the pain or humiliation, and add to one's sense of self-loathing. Two, is to strike back viciously, accuse the joker of being a jackass, and risk looking like a dweeb who can't handle "harmless humor." But the third option is the first rule of positive humor etiquette.

A Consenting-Adult Humor Contract

Danny Mora is Mexican; I'm Irish. He's about five feet nothing and one-half; I'm a towering five feet eight inches tall. Dan has hair, lots of hair, too much hair, he has hair in places where most people don't even have skin; I have less hair than that. Dan's a great cook, and I'm a great eater. I'm humorous; he's funny. We're friends. We trust and care about each other. But it didn't start like that. When we met, I was jealous of his experience, wit, connections, and nifty beret. He was jealous of my enormous talent and my car. As it became obvious that we were going to work together, we established what I refer to as a *Consenting-Adult Humor Contract.*

In healthy management terms, such as the men and women I mentioned at the beginning of this chapter, and in successful families like the Baribaults, informal consenting humor contracts often evolve as a means of processing the inevitable tension that accompanies togetherness. Here's how to build one from scratch.

Step 1: You Talk About It

First, Dan and I talked about the fact that we often relieve tension by making jokes; some of those jokes can be harsh and apparently abusive.

Step 2: Set Limits

I can make fun of your ethnic background, your height, your temper, your gastric distress (you get gastric; the world gets distressed), and your so-called career. *You* can make fun of my ethnicity, baldness, indecision, so-called career, and obsession with new shoes.

If either of us goes too far, we have a signal that lets the other know he has crossed the line. (He slaps my face; I stomp on his flat feet.) No. It's simpler. It's just a matter of saying: "Too far," and we stop. If we feel it's necessary, we discuss what the *too far* is about, so that we won't hurt or offend each other in the future.

We establish environmental limits, such as back off the ethnic stuff when we are with people who don't know us well, because they might not understand that we are kidding.

We respect, without need for explanation, any limits that are important to the other.

A Consenting-Adult Humor Contract resolves problems before they begin. Setting up the rules helps us get to know each other and allays any suspicion that we intend to use joking to camouflage abuse.

In the workplace, such rules are particularly essential. Rather than being established by corporate policy, humor contracts are successful when they are set up by employees who work together.

Step 3: Accept Refusal

Not everybody enjoys oral banter. My wife—who insists she is not unique in her attitude toward teasing—refuses to accept a Consenting-Adult Humor Contract. Though she doesn't mind ribbing at times, she resents it at others "Teasing gives me flashbacks," she says. (It takes her back to childhood, and being jeered at for belonging to the *wrong* religion.)

Tease her at your own risk. When men tell sexist jokes in her presence, she will, as Miss Manners suggests, ask them to explain *precisely* what they mean by the joke. By their answer, she will determine her reply to the humorists. (Admittedly, when friends tell equally offensive sexist jokes, she usually laughs and tries to think of something offensive to say to them.)

If an acquaintance tells a racist joke in her presence, she will again ask for an explanation of exactly what the joke is supposed to mean. She will push and probe until everyone is uncomfortable. Usually, people avoid telling her racist jokes a second time. (With people who *can't* restrain themselves from telling bad jokes of all kinds, she pretends to fall into a state of catalepsy until the offending joke is finished.)

Oh, I forgot about timing. Comic timing comes from the ability to be in the moment, not in your script; it is the ability to listen. It is the same for everyday positive humor. Pay attention. Just because something strikes you as amusing doesn't mean that now is the time to share it.

The Art of Blowing off Steam

Many of my company's clients are hospital and healthcare organizations. I've spent more than enough time studying behavior in emergency rooms, observing operations, and sitting in on that most terrifying hospital event, the hospital committee meeting. It is impossible to work in a hospital and not rely heavily on *something* to relieve the stress of daily life-and-death tension, especially in the emergency room. At times, that something is "black humor."

My experience is that the crisis environment lacking comic relief is often unsafe. In these environments, Terminal Professionalism rules, and can become a contagion.

Unless you have worked in places where life, death, trauma, pain, and terror are common—as on the police force, in the publishing business, or as a junior high school teacher—please try to suspend your judgment.

If you do work in such surroundings, my advice is, beware of the accidental audience. You may feel the need to make a tacky joke about hypochondriac patients to one of your coworkers, while, unknown to either of you, a woman on the other side of the curtain waits for news about her husband who just had a heart attack. Your relief then becomes her burden. It's a hard line to walk, and an easy one to trip on. When you do trip, apologize, forgive yourself, and get back to work.

You can also make use of Humaerobic forms of comic relief that are not likely to offend others. A nurse I know carries her strip of Photo Funnies wherever she goes. A pilot carries his Center of the Universe mug in the cockpit on every flight. A cop gets up early to Howl for Joy with her family. Although casual observers may consider you silly to do these exercises, at least they'll never think you're mean.

One Last Rule: What's up, Doc?

Pure and simple. What do you hope to achieve by joking, kidding, goofing around, playing, or having fun with others? What is your motive? If you have any doubts about positive and negative humor, you can use the etiquette table as a barometer of motive. Just remember one ironclad rule: If you pay attention to others' needs and feelings, you will rarely be guilty of letting bad timing turn positive into negative humor.

Etiquette Table	
Healing humor	*Harmful humor*
Bonds us in understanding or accepting difficulty and responsibility.	**Divides** us from one another and places blame on others.
Laughs at itself.	**Laughs** only at others.
Illuminates solutions.	**Obscures** solutions.
Decreases tension.	**Increases** tension.
Builds confidence.	**Destroys** someone's self-worth.
Involves others in enjoyment.	**Excludes** others from enjoyment.

9. Why Do They Call It Happy Hour? Humor and Substance Abuse

The Laugh Lapse

For the alcoholic, drinking has (or once had) specific functions and pleasures, and giving it up can make him or her feel helpless and miserable. A woman I know said about quitting drink: "It was like giving up my best friend—the one who was always there, who took away my self-consciousness, who made me laugh." She added, "When I resigned myself to getting sober, I was sure that I would never have any real fun again. Thank God, I was wrong."

Although there's nothing funny about alcoholism or substance abuse—except that the absurdities in addictive behavior can help people confront their illness and cherish sobriety—two important relationships connect humor and recovery. One is that humor skills are usually a waste of time *unless* the alcoholic can first achieve sobriety. The second is that without humor skills, recovering from addiction is about as appealing as hopping into the hot tub when you've got a second-degree sunburn.

Drunkalogic

For thousands of years people have used alcohol as a substitute for genuine lightheartedness and exuberance, which is why to this day taverns so frequently refer to 4:00 to 6:00 P.M. as *Happy Hour* rather than Booze Break. In the 1939 text of the AA program, *Alcoholics Anonymous,* Dr. William D. Silkworth wrote that "Men and women drink essentially because they like the effect produced by alcohol." The same holds true today. In a recent Gallup survey, people's top reasons for drinking were increased sociability, relaxation, and personal enjoyment.

For about 90 percent of the population, alcohol is a friend. When life is stressful, the average person can safely take a couple of drinks and feel better and certainly less inhibited—fear of foolishness declines by the drink. In other words, alcohol opens the door to humor *without* requiring people to work at learning specific skills. Even slightly under the influence, most drinkers speak with relative clarity, drive safely (or not at all), and refrain from offensive or dangerous acts.

And, then, there are the *alcoholics.*

Clean and Sober

Before going further, I offer one caveat. Drug use as much as alcoholic drinking gets in the way of finding the real benefits of humor. Some experts will disagree, but throughout this chapter, when I say *sober,* I mean (as they say in California) *clean and sober*. The recovering alcoholic who continues to play around with "recreational drugs" does not quite *grok* what sobriety is about. Alcohol differs from other drugs in that it's legal for some people, but not for others; it's addictive for some individuals, not for others; it is socially unacceptable in most Muslim and Buddhist traditions; and it's messier to snort than cocaine. But dwelling on the differences between the "pure" alcoholic and the "pure" drug abuser can be a trap for people who are trying to recover.

Since 1977, 27 percent of people entering Alcoholics Anonymous have been polydrug users (which does not mean that they snort polyester but that they use lots of different drugs). There is a real danger that when abusers quit drugs, their drinking will increase to compensate. Even more common in the eighties and nineties are alcoholics who have quit drinking but continue to smoke pot, sniff cocaine, drop barbiturates, dabble with speed, and play around with other mood-altering fumes, vapors, potions, and pills.

I Drink Therefore I Are

In Greece, the ancients held drunken orgies in honor of Dionysus, the god of wine. In Rome, the Bacchanalia was an orgiastic festival in which participants caroused in honor of (guess who?) Bacchus.

But drunkenness should *not* be confused with alcoholism. Anybody who can keep liquor down can get drunk, and is likely to do so as long as intoxication is in harmony with prevailing social custom. The average 150-pound person will experience relaxation, slight exhilaration, and lower inhibitions after one quick drink. After two drinks, reaction time slows and muscle control as well as judgment become impaired. Dumb jokes start to seem hilarious. To be funny, Scott and Zelda Fitzgerald got drunk, collected all the women's purses at a Hollywood party, and boiled them, reports biographer Aaron Lathem in *Crazy Sundays.* Three drinks: the drinker has an increasing lack of inhibitions along with impaired ability to make intelligent decisions. With three to four drinks, a person reaches legal intoxication, and shoelaces become funny.

The issue is not whether drink and drugs should exist, but what happens when users lose control. Substances aren't the problem. (Would we have a problem in a world supplied with addictive substances, but where no human beings lived? If a marijuana plant toppled in the forest, and nobody heard it fall, would somebody still get arrested?)

The only thing alcoholics need to have in common is that booze and drugs have created serious problems for them. I have known people who drink only once a year, but who nevertheless have a serious problem because they cannot predictably control their behavior once they take the first drink. I have known others who drink moderately every day, but their drinking doesn't impair their social, emotional, physical, or spiritual well-being. Alcoholism is not a matter of quantity, frequency, intensity, or even obvious outward effects; it's an issue of context and consequences.

The picture of an addict is as diverse as the cultures, families, and personal experiences of the human race. (Some drunks are even—I know it's hard to believe—bald.)

When it comes to addressing the difficulties created by such individuals, the task can seem overwhelming. But it is a problem that can be solved one alcoholic at a time. Here are some facts that can help us understand why the disease genuinely is every American's business.

What's Alcoholism? As with so many things in life, it depends on whom you ask. These definitions are *all* accepted by various authorities.

- Alcoholism is any use of alcoholic beverages that causes any damage to the individual or to society or both.—E. M. Jellinek, father of the disease theory of alcoholism

- Drug dependence of the alcohol type may be said to exist when the consumption of alcohol by an individual exceeds the limits that are accepted by his culture, if he consumes alcohol at times that are deemed inappropriate within that culture, or his intake of alcohol becomes so great as to injure his health or impair his social relationships.—World Health Organization, revised definition

- Alcoholism is an illness characterized by significant impairment that is directly associated with persistent and excessive use of alcohol. Impairment may involve physiological, psychological, or social dysfunction.—American Medical Association

Ten percent of the population is *alcoholic*, and therefore can never *safely* take the first drink. (Ten percent is a moderate estimate; some researchers say it is more like 5 percent or 7 percent, and others estimate alcoholism to be as high as 15 percent.) The problem is that as life tensions increase and the onus of drinking or drugging is lessened, the percentage of the population exposed to alcohol and drugs expands.

As exposure increases, so too does the number of people who become abusers.

Nor do the effects of alcoholism end with the alcoholic. In the United States, seven million children under age eighteen are affected by a parent's alcoholism. Twenty-two million American adults grew up in alcoholic homes. Alcoholism affects every life partner of the conservatively estimated ten million alcoholics in the United States, and every alcoholic affects at least one close friend or a colleague at work. Therefore, the number of Americans whose lives are directly influenced by alcoholism is likely to be about eighty million.

- **Alcohol is the number one drug problem among young people.**

- **Alcohol hits women harder and faster than it does men.**

- **It may take younger people ten to fifteen years to develop alcoholism, but the illness can devastate elders in "a few months to a year or two."** In a 1989 Pacific Northwest Extension publication on the use of alcohol, experts say that moderate amounts of alcohol can cause temporary or permanent dementia in the elderly. Elders "metabolize alcohol and other drugs less efficiently," according to Frank Baumeister, M.D., of Portland, Oregon. "The margin between a safe level and a toxic level becomes narrower."

- **Recent evidence shows that alcoholism is triggered by internal and external influences, including a predisposition to the disease that can be genetically inherited.** The chances of becoming alcoholic increase radically for those of us with blood relatives who are alcoholics. Biological sons of alcoholic males have four times the average rate of alcoholism, even when they are raised by nonalcoholic adoptive parents, according to Lester Grinspoon, M.D., and James B. Bakalar, J.D.

- **Cultural and ethnic origins, too, make a difference.** In France, alcohol is consumed at any time of day, and intoxication is socially acceptable; the French have the world's highest rate of alcoholism. Jewish and Italian cultures, which have traditionally frowned upon intoxication and have seen drink only as part of a dining experience, have a very low rate of alcoholism. In China, moderation is valued, resulting in a low rate of alcoholism there. The Irish? With my heritage, the less said the better.

- **Because drinking lowers people's inhibitions, it allows them to commit acts that would be unthinkable under normal circumstances.** Alcohol is a factor in:

  - 50 percent of arrests
  - 80 percent of murders
  - 70 percent of serious assaults
  - 50 percent of forcible rapes
  - 72 percent of robberies
  - 50 percent of family disputes in which the police are involved.

- In America, **alcoholism results in greater healthcare costs than all respiratory diseases and cancers combined!** And as for drug use? According to Partnership for a Drug-Free America, **one in six workers**

is impaired by drugs. "The hazards of illegal drugs extend far beyond the individual user," explains the Partnership. "Your drug-impaired employee is not just a danger to himself. He's also a threat to fellow workers. Studies show that drug-related industrial accidents involving both users and non-users are increasing."

Of Course, You Don't Have a Problem

Denial. I don't deny anything! I didn't sleep under bridges. I didn't drink first thing in the morning. I didn't get any driving under the influence summonses. Okay, I got one. But just one. (Heck, anybody could have one problem while driving intoxicated, right?) I held a job—lots of them. I was successfully married—several times. I had a few blackouts, not many, at widely separated periods. I think . . . But . . . but . . . but . . .

Alcoholism, more than any other illness, is referred to as a disease of denial. Therefore the more likely you are to be an alcoholic, the more reasons you will find to believe it can't be true.

How does denial work? In *The Facts About Drinking*, the author says, "The alcoholic knows that his or her drinking creates major problems, knows how unhappy he or she is making others, and is aware that he or she is the source of great anger and the cause of pain. But the alcoholic denies and minimizes the drinking and family and friends share the denial, deluding themselves into believing that the person is not an alcoholic. The label *alcoholic* is seen by many to be worse than the drunkenness, the hurt inflicted, the loss of livelihood, and the physical deterioration."

Why do alcoholics so frequently deny the obvious fact of their disease? Dr. Vaillant and other experts explain that denial is a highly effective *defense mechanism*—an unconscious negation of reality that protects sick people from the pain of recognition. Unlike optimists who choose to focus on the positive, the alcoholic denies the problem. The lengths to which substance abusers go to deny they have a problem are often darkly humorous. Such people will cling to the last vestiges of even semisober behavior to prove they are *fine* because:

> "B.S.! I don't remember having any blackouts!"
>
> "Most great writers are drunks; you want me to quit and blow my chances?"
>
> "Hey, we both know that alcoholics are just people who drink more than their doctors do."
>
> "I drink beer and wine, not the hard stuff."
>
> "If you had my problems, you'd get drunk and sit in a closet all weekend, too."
>
> "I have a job, I eventually pay my bills, and I hardly ever wreck the car."
>
> "Alcoholic? Me? Listen to this: Piter Peeper poked a pike of purkle poppers. So there."

The point that I failed to understand, for years, was that nonalcoholics didn't need to make up excuses.

Yes, We Have No Denial

Family members, friends, and coworkers all can participate in the deathtrap of denial. I'll never forget as a kid being at a friend's house when his Mom had been knocking back scotches for two hours before dinner. She babbled incoherently through the salad course, and passed out face first in the soup. Nobody at the table moved!

"What's wrong with her?" I asked nervously, as she blew bubbles in the chowder.

"Nothing," the others said, almost in unison.

Then the woman's husband muttered something about his wife's fatigue as he gently lifted her face from the bowl and turned her head to rest on the tablecloth. Everyone kept eating as though nothing unusual had happened. Denial can be so powerful that it allows people close to the alcoholic to view reality in a way that supports the alcoholic's need to believe things are just fine.

Coworkers who cover for the alcoholic are frequently good at denial, too. These people tell themselves that they didn't *really* see what they saw, and don't *really* know what they know. Frequently, they suppress their knowledge of a friend's alcoholism in the mistaken belief that they are being helpful. Most of these friends don't understand that by allowing the self-destructive behavior to continue unchallenged they are helping the substance abuser to destroy a career, a family, maybe even a life or two.

The people I charmed, conned, or stumbled past in my drinking days were helping me get sicker. To make informed decisions about how to solve my problems, I needed the truth (such as what I had really done in those blackouts, or that drinking made me an obnoxious jerk.) The drinking pals I hung out with certainly confirmed that I was a fine fellow, but then, I went to great lengths to drink with people who drank the way I did.

My own family surely loved me, and some of them still doubt that I really was an alcoholic. After all, I quit drinking didn't I? In my family you were an alcoholic only if you died with a drink in your hand. By not allowing drinkers to experience the consequences of their substance abuse, the problem is postponed until it is so severe that recovery may be impossible.

Step 1: What? Me Worry?

Is alcohol creating a problem in your life? If so, the first step is to admit it. Ideally, you will not have to lose self-respect, a home, a family, a job, or most of your sanity before you realize that you're out of control.

Answer these twelve questions from the AA pamphlet, "Is AA for You?" as honestly as you can. Remember, only you can decide whether you need help and only you need to see the answers. (If you don't want to take this test, you probably need it.)

1. Have you decided to stop drinking for a week or so, but lasted only a couple of days?
2. Do you wish people would mind their own business about your drinking—stop telling you what to do?
3. Have you ever switched from one kind of drink to another in the hope that this would keep you from getting drunk?
4. Have you had to have an eye-opener upon awakening during the past year?
5. Do you envy people who can drink without getting into trouble?
6. Have you had problems connected with drinking during the past year?
7. Has your drinking caused trouble at home?

8. Do you ever try to get "extra" drinks at a party because you do not get enough?
9. Do you tell yourself you can stop drinking any time you want to, even though you keep getting drunk when you don't mean to?
10. Have you missed days of work or school because of drinking?
11. Do you have "blackouts"?
12. Have you ever felt that your life would be better if you did not drink?

(*Questions from "Is AA for You?" reprinted with permission of AA, World Services, Inc. Use of this material does not mean that AA has reviewed or approved the contents of this publication.*)

According to Alcoholics Anonymous, if you have answered yes four or more times, you probably have trouble with alcohol. For more information about alcoholism and AA, see the list of addresses at the end of this chapter.

Abstinence Makes the Tight Go Ponder

My experience and subsequent work with alcoholics leads me to conclude that, for the alcoholic, consumption of alcohol and "mind-altering" drugs is not only risky, but can eventually erode the capacity for humor or joy. (I mean the so-called recreational drugs, *not* responsibly prescribed medications.) I have buried more people than I care to remember who went out drinking to "have a good time."

Although alcoholics may convince themselves that their drinking is caused by emotional problems or some catastrophe, experts insist that "people who drink merely to relieve anxiety or console themselves for what is lost or missing in their lives will stop when alcohol no longer provides relief or consolation." In sharp contrast, when alcoholics "drink to forget their troubles, the troubles are brought on by drinking. Misunderstanding this may encourage the tendency of some alcoholics to deny the real source of their misery," explain Grinspoon and Bakalar in the *Harvard Medical School Mental Health Review.*

Quitting for a while—even a long while—doesn't necessarily solve the problem. My friend Paul quit after one bout of blackout drinking at age sixteen. He abstained until he retired at age sixty-five and started a furniture-making hobby. He began to nip a bit of brandy "to take the edge off the feeling that because I'd retired, I was worthless."

It did not take long for the brandy to nip back. Before his sixty-seventh birthday, Paul's combination of drinking and woodworking had cost him dearly. "I cut off the first finger a month after I began working in my garage," he told me. "I just chalked it off to old age. Whacked the second one off just a month later. Damned glad a friend of mine suggested treatment when he did."

Whether or not a given expert believes that alcoholism is a disease, most of them agree that for alcoholics who have become "serious enough to require admission to an alcoholism clinic, returning to moderate drinking is rarely possible." Permanent *abstinence* is the appropriate treatment. When several studies sought to prove that alcoholics could be "taught" to control their drinking, the results were unfortunate. In 1969, researchers Mark and Linda Sobell "trained" twenty alcoholics to drink responsibly. Their report caused a wave of outrage from proponents of abstinence. One of them, alcoholism counselor Mary Pendery, conducted a follow-up study. Pendery discovered that thirteen of the Sobells' twenty "trained" alcoholics had been readmitted to treatment within a year of the study. Ten years after the treatment, researchers found that "nine of the patients in the controlled drinking group were still alcoholic, six were abstinent, and four were dead. Only one could be regarded as a moderate drinker."

But why can't alcoholics be taught to drink normally?

The answer may lie in the so-called progressiveness of the disease, or the genetic and metabolic differences between alcoholics and other people. I understand that answering this question may prove important in deterring alcoholism, but I don't think it's necessary to figure out which bullet will miss its mark, which will only wound, and which will kill, before deciding to unload the gun. Regardless of the cause, the results are the same—when alcoholics drink, sooner or later they are likely to harm themselves and others.

A Light Heart at the End of the Tunnel

How is a newly abstinent alcoholic supposed to deal with stress resulting from the distance between life's pressures and his or her ability to handle them? For me, the answer lay in acquiring tools that I could use to reduce stress. Because I had started to drink at age twelve, so early that I had hardly any experience in using healthy adult coping mechanisms, I had to experience emotional adolescence starting at age thirty-six. Until sobriety, alcohol had been my stress-management program, and the only fluidity I knew came out of a bottle. Without it, at first, I felt overwhelmed by loneliness, confusion, and sadness.

At the Center for Attitudinal Healing, I first discovered that *community* was essential to healing. It turned out to be crucial in healing alcoholism and drug abuse as well. In preceding chapters I have explained that a sense of connection to community has been important to survival for POWs, hostages, cancer patients, and other people in crisis. Within the safety and warmth of community, friendships can be nurtured, especially if the community consists of people who have similar problems and solutions.

In his investigations, Dr. Vaillant identified four components necessary in effectively treating alcoholism. They are:

1. Treatment must offer an effective, nonchemical substitute behavior for alcohol dependence.
2. Treatment must suggest something other than willpower to remind the alcoholic to stay sober (such as Antabuse).
3. Treatment must provide the means for repairing social and medical damage.
4. Treatment must restore both self-esteem and hope.

After comparing four remedies, including Alcoholics Anonymous (AA), hospitalization, Antabuse (a medication that causes illness rather than intoxication when the alcoholic tries to drink), psychotherapy, and tranquilizers, Vaillant concluded that the simplest means of providing all four components was membership in AA "or its reasonable equivalent."

In AA and similar groups, the alcoholics find "gentle peer support." They are also exposed to truly successful people who provide a "substitute gratification that takes the place of dependence on drinking and the barroom." Vaillant explains that, "unlike clinic hours, AA meetings compete with barroom hours."

One AA friend of mine described the program as an extended family that has branches everywhere. "In the city where I live, I can choose from hundreds of meetings each week," she said. "When I travel, I can find meetings and feel at home anywhere in the world." Currently, AA has more than 85,000 groups in 112 countries. The program reaches 650,000 alcoholics yearly in the United States alone. "It's an enormous fellowship, united by common beliefs and goals—but without dogma."

Vaillant says that AA provides members with the advantage of "belonging to a group of caring but abstinent individuals who have found solutions to the typical problems that beset the newly sober alcoholic. . . . " The group helps relieve the newcomer's loneliness while encouraging better self-care. Older members assist newer ones in acquiring simple skills that are essential for developing *friendships*—the ability to converse, to stop lying to others and to themselves. With all this, humor skills can help.

Finally, the AA community teaches the alcoholic to regain a sense of self-respect and value through active altruism, another of the healthy coping mechanisms I encountered at the Center for Attitudinal Healing. Alcoholics who are willing to share have improved odds of personal recovery, because giving knowledge away secures it while enhancing its worth.

Humor in Recovery

One of my primary aims here is to reach the people who abandon sobriety because they are convinced that it can't be fun. "Many alcoholics feel a void in their lives after they stop drinking," say authors Monti, Abrams, Kadden, and Cooney in *Treating Alcohol Dependence.* They point out that in lives primarily composed of eating, sleeping, working, and drinking, when the drinking stops, people are left with nothing but routine. And, often, "the absence of pleasant leisure activities" becomes a crucial problem for the sober alcoholic.

Fortunately, in my own recovery, I met clean and sober people who proved by their example that it was possible to rediscover the will to live and a sense of fun. Much of their humor arose from self-discovery, release from fear and anger, and camaraderie.

In sobriety, along with learning from others, I was able to put to use humor skills I had learned years earlier. As long as I'd had access to drink and drugs, I'd put off working at feeling good, telling myself that fun was a luxury. Sober, however, I became keenly aware that joyousness is a developed skill that we must use or lose—that failing to reclaim our right to those humor skills can have devastating consequences for recovering substance abusers.

Step 1: Accessing Absurdity in Addiction

I really didn't want to be an alcoholic. I'd had a hard life, I thought. Now this. "Why me?" I complained to a man who had many years of sobriety.

"Why not you?" he wisecracked. "You're not the Center of the Universe; far as I can see, you're not even the center of town."

My friend had helped me to recall that some people are alcoholics, just as some people are tall, some have cancer, and some inherit billions of dollars from relatives who hated them. In short, life is not particularly fair, but knowing how to use your sense of humor can get you by.

Still, it took months before I could discover the *humor* in my own history. Although I heard people laughing about their insane thinking and behavior while drunk, none of that seemed funny. Were they idiots, or what? I felt like crying as I discovered that I had never really drowned my sorrows (because alcohol is a preservative, you see). My troubles, apparently, had been pickled and stored, hidden on some shadowy back shelf of my memory.

I stayed with my recovery group but I doubted I'd ever laugh. And yet, only three months later, I told friends this story about an incident from my drinking days:

One morning—some year in the late seventies—I awoke in a room I didn't recognize, apparently a basement. I heard voices upstairs. After waiting a few moments for my mind to clear, I still could not figure out where I was. I did, however, remember a phone number. Using the phone nearest at hand, I dialed the number. It was my home phone. I got my answering machine, telling me that I wasn't in right then, but if I would leave a message for myself, I would get back to me as soon as possible. In all sincerity, and with what seemed like superb logic, I left a message for me to call me and tell me where I was. Then I hung up and waited for me to call me back. When I later found that message on my machine, I couldn't remember having left it.

My humor perspective was finally kicking in because the memory struck me as wonderfully absurd. That I had managed to rationalize such behavior was unbelievable and truly, truly funny. Being able to laugh allowed me to confront and overcome the pain. My past was no longer in control. I was.

Today, when shameful memories or old behaviors recur, I do my best to confront them by finding the humor in the situation. Humor helps me to detach—with pleasure, a state of mind that makes it possible to determine appropriate action. **Once I can laugh at my problem, I gain control; and, for a moment, I am free.**

Although recovering alcoholics need help in growing up after years of social retardation, they need just as badly to learn how to play—sober. **Humor is a substitute replacing the need for substances to cope with stress, society, strangers, and sickness.** I try to keep a hoard of touchstones—clown noses, fright masks—that remind me to smile when I begin to take myself too seriously.

Step 2: Self Lightly, Sauce Seriously

After my friends helped me to find the absurdity in my history of substance abuse, the next step was to separate me from the substance, and not just by not drinking it. When I sobered up, I was left contemplating a history of deceits, abandonments, injuries, and mistakes that swamped me in guilt. Three things helped me realize that I was not a monster but *just* a person who had a disease called alcoholism.

First, I got to know other recovering alcoholics who had successfully overcome their illness. Second, I followed the simple instructions they had used to recover, one of which required figuring out my mistakes in life and making an effort to rectify them. (Oh, rapture. What fun.) Alcoholics who belong to AA and some other support groups actually write a "moral inventory" and read it to a trusted friend or adviser.

Step 3: A Sense of Joy in Sobriety

Once the alcoholic *has* quit drinking or drugging or both, humor skills can help smooth the transition into a satisfying sobriety. It may sound impossible, but if you are an addict or alcoholic, you *can* learn to have fun sober. What the addict has been looking for in booze—good times and relief from fear, anger, despair, and loneliness—can be found in recovery.

Seriously, sober doesn't have to be somber. Because I expected sobriety to be tedious, I was surprised to learn that not only could I have fun without alcohol but, better yet, I could remember it!

Slowly, everything in my life got better, not worse. But, because I'd achieved so little real joy in life, I had to start from scratch.

One tool that recovering substance abusers can benefit from is the Joy List detailed in Chapter 6. It really provides an opportunity to start learning about life from a semiadult perspective.

Step 4: Kiss Your Fear of Foolishness Goodbye

Without alcohol the newly sober person may feel overwhelmed by gawkiness. After all, a substance that, by altering the brain's chemical balance, can turn introverts into wild extroverts, is not easily replaced by coffee or soda pop. For most people it is horrifying to sober up in the body of an adult with the social and emotional graces of an adolescent. For someone who has relied on drinking to socialize, a cocktail party with nothing to drink but orange juice can be pretty traumatic.

Humaerobics, the physical exercises described in earlier chapters, can be particularly helpful here. The Shake 'n' Face, a Howl for Joy, an American Bat Face, or even a few Stand, Breathe and Smile repetitions, can help many recovering addicts get back in touch with their physical ability to express feeling good—sober. Or before going to a party, take a look at the Photo Funnies I suggested you create back in Chapter 3. You've already made a fool of yourself, so why not lighten up?

Humor and Helping

You may be wondering about your own relationship to alcohol and drugs. If substance abuse is causing a problem in any part of your life, a number of profit and nonprofit organizations are set up exclusively to help people deal with addiction. Take advantage of them. Remember, the alcoholic is not a bad person trying to *get good,* but a sick person trying to get well. Until that illness is overcome, the capacity for a real sense of joy in life, for loving relationships, for a sense of humor, is simply zero.

If you're nonalcoholic but live with, work with, employ, or are related to an alcoholic whose behavior worries you, be aware that suggesting he or she ought to "develop some willpower," or "start thinking positive," will often provide him or her with yet another excuse to keep drinking. (Nobody understands me. Better have another cocktail . . . sniff, sniff . . . pour me.)

What *is* the solution?

First, I strongly recommend that you refuse to cover for the alcoholic or drug addict, and, second, promptly contact the experts for sources of additional help. Here's a list of some of them.

Help!

Alcoholics Anonymous,
General Services Organization
P.O. Box 459, Grand Central Station
New York, NY 10163
(212) 686-1100

A free, international self-help organization. For local information, see the White Pages in your telephone book.

Al-Anon Family Group Headquarters
P.O. Box 182, Madison Square Station
New York, NY 10010
(800) 356-9996

Al-Anon is a free, self-help organization with 30,000 groups worldwide. For local information, see your telephone White Pages.

Institute on Black Chemical Abuse
2616 Nicollet Avenue South
Minneapolis, MN 55408
(612) 871-7878

This institute provides assistance to programs seeking to serve African-American clients and others of color with increased effectiveness.

**National Clearinghouse for Alcohol and
  Drug Information**
P.O. Box 2345
Rockville, MD 20852
(301) 468-2600

*This organization provides a publication list and
placement on a mailing list. Single copies are free.*

National Council on Alcoholism, Inc.
12 West 21st Street
New York, NY 10010
(212) 206-6770; or (800) 622-2255 (24-hour 7-day information line)

A voluntary health agency with 300 local affiliates.

Narcotics Anonymous
World Service Office
P.O. Box 9999
Van Nuys, CA 91409
(818) 780-3951

International self-help organization similar to AA.

> *We came to meadows full of flowers. We saw*
> *and realized that they were there, but we had*
> *no feelings about them. . . .*
> —*Viktor E. Frankl*, **Man's Search**
> **for Meaning**

10. What's So Funny? The Absence of Humor

Dark Side of the Moon

In this chapter I mean to help you deal with "normal" reactions such as short-term sadness, loss, bad days, bad weather, bad news, bad backs, the blues, PMS, and IRS. But true clinical depression is a more serious matter that we also need to talk about, because like alcohol, depression gets in the way of humor, and nowhere can humor be more dangerously misapplied than in dealing with this illness. Even in its early stages, depression makes it difficult or impossible for people to lighten up. Trying to treat depression with humor can backfire and increase people's sense of isolation and despair.

Where then do humor skills enter into coping with depression? Humor does *not* alleviate clinical depression or any other mental illness, but when humor reappears, it usually signals the beginning of recovery.

Fill in the Blanks

Although this test is by no means an absolute indicator of whether or not you are depressed, it is a beginning diagnostic tool.

1. Do you awaken early in the morning or during the night and spend time unable to return to sleep? Or do you spend long periods in bed, not wanting to get up? Yes_____ No_____

2. Do you feel nervous and irritable in a way that is not your usual self? Yes_____ No_____

3. Do you have difficulty in concentrating that keeps you from performing tasks that before were quite simple? Yes_____ No_____

4. Have you had a change in appetite, either eating too much and not enjoying it or not feeling like eating at all? Yes_____ No_____

5. Do ideas begin to prey on your mind and seem impossible to turn off, so that your mind just keeps racing and racing? Yes_____ No_____

6. Do you feel sad, angry, or more irritable in ways uncharacteristic of your usual state? Yes_____ No_____

If the answer to any of these questions is yes, you may have a problem with depression. If the answer to three or more of them is affirmative, seek professional assistance. Understand that depression is *not* a weakness of spirit or character. It is an illness.

If you live with depression, this chapter can help you understand a bit more about the ailment, and humor skills can help as you begin to rise from the darkness. But please, if you have *any* suspicion that you are depressed, don't wait to get help until it's so evident that you no longer believe in solutions.

Minor Morose Mood Management

What then *isn't* depression? That's important, too. Many of us get up in the morning and say, "I'm depressed," when we really mean, "I think I'm about to have a bad day," or, "I need a new mattress," or, "If I live, I'll never eat at that restaurant again."

If you feel down in the dumps, or like singing the blues, or even sadder than a vegetarian dog in a butcher shop, but lack the indicators of depression listed earlier, humor skill development is probably just the ticket.

Bad days do not have to have a cause; in fact, they usually don't. The blues, which are slightly different but equally common in human experience, are generally triggered by loss—lost hopes, lost dreams, lost love, or lost friends. When you have a bad day, you can enjoy yourself by wallowing in your misery, or you can, quite appropriately, use humor skills and tools to kick the mood. Here are some guidelines:

Rule 1: You Have a Right to Have a Bad Day

If the world were perfect and an angel appeared every morning at your bedside with celestial coffee and your *Daily List of Proper Actions,* you'd still have bad days. Nobody knows why these daily mood fluctuations occur, although multitudes make money on our desire for a simple answer.

Have a bad day, then, **but don't blame anyone for it.** It is not *their* fault. If you have to blame someone,

blame the Hittites, because none are left to feel offended.

Rule 2: Let Others Know You Are Having a Bad Day

I have a "bad-day" button: *Back off: Fish Breath*. I
wear this warning on my lapel so that people in my
office know they should not take offense at my small-
mindedness that day.

I have another button I like for similar occasions:
Recent studies prove I don't have to be reasonable.
When strangers ask me what the buttons are about,
I complain. They never ask twice. This method allows
me to stew and fret until the need passes; oddly, the
need passes quickly when I acknowledge my bad day.

Rule 3: You Have the Option to Dispense with Bad Days When You Choose To

It's simple. When you're shambling around the house
in the morning, doing your impression of Oscar the
Grouch, test the staying power of your incipient bad
day by doing some Humaerobics. Stand in front of the
mirror for a few moments and make the most absurd
faces you can. Howl for joy. Do a Shake 'n' Face series.
If those things make you feel nastier, stop. If the exercises begin to crack your gloom, do some more.

Put on your Mickey Mouse underwear, or go wild
and wear your T-shirt backward. Challenge your bad
day and see if you really want to hold on to it. Wear
your clown nose on the drive to work. Top off your
snazzy business attire with a beat-up baseball cap.

If the bad day doesn't break right away, try starting
over a few times as the day wears on. Check your Joy
List, or take a minivacation. A genuine bad day just
can't stand up to that sort of treatment. Most of all,
stand up to your Fear of Foolishness.

Guidelines for the Blues

Because the blues are connected with a specific loss, they usually won't evaporate as easily as bad days. But you can still take action that allows you to maintain a healthy perspective, cope more effectively, and survive without getting bent out of shape. DO NOT get into the game of denying yourself pleasure as a bizarre, sadistic punishment. Hey! You already feel bad. That's payment enough. Besides, constructing a variety of small, pleasurable coping activities is good for you.

Healthy Pleasures, by Robert Ornstein, Ph.D., and David Sobel, M.D., is a wonderful introduction to the value of feeling good. They cite a study of "self-complexity" in men and women. People who diversify their interests by gathering small but enjoyable activities report "less depression, fewer foul moods, colds, coughs, stomach pains, headaches, and muscle aches than their less complex counterparts."

According to Ornstein and Sobel, if you can invent and pursue a variety of fullfilling activities, the positive effect "is neither sinful nor counterproductive. The positive mood may help you deal better with difficulty."

Here are some activities that have helped me break a blues bummer.

Suggestion 1: I practice my fly-casting techniques in the back yard while listening to an environmental tape of rushing water through earphones with my portable tape player. Last week I caught a two-pound banana slug.

Suggestion 2: I stand on a street corner smiling at strangers. (Careful with this; being nice to strangers is often considered a sign of mental imbalance or a come-on.)

Suggestion 3: I call a supportive friend.

Suggestion 4: I spend time with people who remind me that I have the ability to feel good.

Suggestion 5: I take in a lighthearted movie, or get out of the house and do something else that I enjoy.

Suggestion 6: I read a book by Rabbi Kushner, Elaine Pagels, Jerry Jampolsky, Ram Dass, Joan Borysenko, or Tim Hansel. (For further suggestions, refer to the reading list at the back of this book.)

Suggestion 7: I pull out my Joy List and allow myself to do one or two of the things on it.

Suggestion 8: I remind willing loved ones that they can have fun. When Roma is having a bad day, I draw her into play. Nothing outrageous like forcing her to dress up in a pickle suit or take a walk through K-Mart singing Christmas carols. But we might rent a comedy for the VCR. Or I may encourage her to call old friends. If her response is to glare, shriek, or storm out of the room, then *I* watch a Three Stooges video, or call her friends.

Down 'n' Doubt

But what about depression?

Even medical authors apply the label to everything from "normal" mood fluctuations (you and I might call them rotten days) to psychotic episodes and suicidal obsession. One thing is certain: at its extreme, clinical depression is a "profound sense of despair" that often lasts months, incapacitating its victims, "leaving them unable to work, care for their families, or perform other tasks."

Many, perhaps most of us, experience short-term depressive states following major, stressful events such as a death in the family or loss of a job. With or without treatment, and within a limited time, we usually return to whatever was normal for us prior to the onset of most depressions. If an episode continues, or the symptoms intensify rather than let up, the disorder is then categorized as major depression. It is estimated that about 15 percent of people who experience the illness commit suicide.

According to the *Harvard Guide to Psychiatry,* clinically ill patients can be distinguished from those of normal mood by:

- Disturbances in sleep, appetite, sex drive.
- Reduced desire and ability to perform the usual social roles in the family and workplace, and so on.
- Disturbances in "reality testing" that indicate delusion, hallucination, or confusion.

Like alcoholism, depression is so widespread (it is referred to as the common cold of mental disorders) that it affects nearly everyone in America either directly or indirectly. One of the most thorough studies of depression was conducted for more than a decade by Dr. William Zung, a professor of psychiatry associated with Duke University and the Veterans Administration Medical Center in North Carolina. According to his findings, the National Institute of Mental Health's estimate of *10 million plus depressives* in the United States is, if anything, conservative.

Other current facts and figures include:

- Rates of depression are highest for the unmarried and widowed.

- Women are twice as likely as men to be hit hard by depression.

- Baby boomers show increased incidence of depression.

- The latest statistics indicate that clinical depression costs United States employers $17 billion annually in lost work time.

- A recent study of clinical depression among Westinghouse employees showed that the illness correlates highly with conflict in one's relationship with a supervisor. It's been proven that the more *control* employees have in their occupation, the lower the level of stress. (Remember the enhanced sense of *control* that is one of the prime by-products of the first humor skill—choosing to access absurdity in adversity?)

Pulitzer Prize–winning author William Styron survived a suicidal depression and went on to write about it in *Darkness Visible: A Memoir of Madness*. But even this acclaimed novelist admitted to having difficulty in putting the experience in understandable words. He wrote:

> Depression is a disorder of mood, so mysteriously painful and elusive . . . as to verge close to being beyond description. It thus remains nearly incomprehensible to those who have not experienced it in its extreme mode, although the gloom, "the blues" which people go through occasionally and associate with the general hassle of everyday existence are of such prevalence that they do give many individuals a hint of the illness in its catastrophic form. But at the time of which I write I had descended far past those familiar, manageable doldrums.

By the Numbers

In *Darkness Visible,* Styron expresses astonishment at how, when his reflections on depression appeared in *The New York Times,* the response was an immense outpouring from fellow sufferers, all expressing gratitude at finding out how common their affliction was. Because telling anyone about an experience of depression is often met with glib advice, such as "Come on, it's a great world, pull yourself out of it," millions of people feel compelled to deny or hide their pain.

In part, Styron's story is significant because it shows that even severe depression can be beaten and nightmares of madness endured until the dreamer eventually awakens to reclaim a sense of joy.

Causes, Conditions, and Cures

On May 4, 1988, psychiatrist Lewis L. Judd, director of the National Institute of Mental Health (NIMH) began a campaign to inform Americans about the symptoms and treatment of clinical depression. One point Judd wished to emphasize was that depression is not a "passing mood or a sign of personal weakness."

In fact, depression is an illness with multiple causes. Heredity greatly influences whether an individual becomes depressed. According to the *Harvard Medical School Mental Health Letter,* "In families of patients with major depression or bipolar illness, the rate of depression is at least two or three times the average. Twenty-five percent of patients with major depression and up to 50 percent of patients with bipolar disorder have a relative with some form of mood disorder, mild or severe."

Medical experts believe that many cases of major depression result from a biochemical imbalance in the brain. Although most people react negatively when they are subjected to stress, the bad mood usually passes—which is fortunate given today's ever-rising stress levels. If the stress continues too long, or is too severe, or if a person is biologically predisposed, the bad mood develops into the disease of depression.

Finding the right treatment for a person, though far more likely now than twenty or even ten years ago, can still be a frustrating task. Styron points out in *Darkness Visible* that his recovery from depression was complicated by many problems, including his expectation that once diagnosed, his cure would be swift. He was cruelly disappointed. Still, NIMH estimates that depression can be treated successfully with antidepressant medication, psychotherapy, or both in 80 to 90 percent of the cases.

Dancing with Demons

Nearly as painful as being depressed is watching helplessly as the illness torments or kills a close friend. The dearer the friend, the more acute one's frustration. Even if you are an experienced psychotherapist, using humor with depressed patients can be dangerous. According to Christian Hageseth III, M.D., it is unwise to apply humor to dealings between therapist and patient until the individual being treated is on the way to recovery.

As Hageseth points out in *A Laughing Place,* in the early stages of treatment, "there is no telling how your attempts at humor might be interpreted—

or misinterpreted." Furthermore, in the early stages of mental disorder, the patient's humor may be a "denial of a problem or a means of evading anxiety."

Later, however, Hageseth adds, "humor may represent insight and positive coping style."

Humor becomes tricky when applied to depressive individuals because the disease is so complex. Among the dozens of symptoms that may indicate a progression from normal sadness to a state of depression, one primary indicator is considered universal. That indicator is inability to enjoy activities that once brought joy or satisfaction, a condition psychiatry calls *anhedonia*. In extreme cases, that which once was pleasurable becomes painful or abhorrent.

With affairs in this state, suggesting to depressed persons that they try to discover the absurdity in their situation, or try to take themselves lightly and their problems seriously, can only make matters worse. For clinically depressed individuals, self-help cures are unlikely. (If you forego using a parachute when jumping from a plane at 35,000 feet, you are unlikely to survive.)

Handling Depression

Rule 1: Get Help

If you suspect that *you* are dealing with depression, seek professional help. If you then find that your feelings of sadness, loss, or melancholy do not fit the definition of depression, the information is worth the investment of time and money. You may be among the few who can arrest depressive symptoms by enlisting help before the ceiling caves in.

Rule 2: Share the Pain

Invest heavily in a support group or community—
spiritual, professional, familial, or group therapy.
Shared problems seem less heavy.

Rule 3: Talk Back and Defend Yourself

Every time the demons tell you that you are skinny,
fat, stupid, ugly, useless, or worthless, try to write
down in a journal statements that refute the negative
messages.

Rule 4: Help Others

Give of yourself as soon as you can (which may not be
soon at all). For some depressed individuals, helping
others takes them out of self and away from their own
pain.

A nonalcoholic friend who had worked for years as a
radio personality volunteered to record books on tape
for the blind. "I'll tell you what," she said. "I put more
emotion into those readings than you can imagine.
Boy, if there was a character who got angry or weepy, I
could work out a lot of feelings. And when I got letters
from people who had heard the tapes and thought they
were brilliant, I laughed. God, that felt good."

Rule 5: What NOT to Do Until the Doctor Comes

If you are depressed, forget about humor skills until
you're feeling better.

Rule 6: If You Wish to Help a Friend

Hageseth suggests that when the person is a friend
of yours, wait until "improvement is clearly evident,
and then go about using this material as you would

with any other friend whose experience of humor you would like to enhance."

Attempting to force depressed people to laugh or "snap out of it" is an act of torment, not treatment. It is like telling someone with no legs that if they would just change their attitude, they would be able to jog.

A Groundhog Speaks of Shadows and Light

I am not the person to tell you if you are clinically depressed. But perhaps my experience, strength, and hope will help one other person hang on long enough to rise from his or her own despair to learn what William Styron recorded upon his own reentry into the light. In this excerpt, the poet he refers to is Dante, who also suffered an apparent lifelong battle with depression:

> For those who have dwelt in depression's dark wood, and known its inexplicable agony, their return from the abyss is not unlike the ascent of the poet, trudging upward and upward into what he saw as "the shining world." There, whoever has been restored to health has almost always been restored to the capacity for serenity and joy, and this may be indemnity enough for having endured the despair beyond despair.
>
> *E quindi uscimmo a riveder le stelle.*
> *And so we came forth, and once again beheld the stars.*

It takes about ten years to get used to how old you are.
—Unknown

11. Talkin' 'bout My Generation: For Sylvie

On the Trail of the Bouncing Chicken

Normally, I enjoyed road trips, meeting new people, and the excitement of helping them lighten up. But on this one afternoon in spring 1985 I was exhausted. My body ached and my head throbbed. The day before, I had presented a full-day seminar, "Humor Skills and Aging," for a national gerontological conference. It had been my fifth workshop in a speaking tour that included four states, three time zones, and five hotels in nine days. That night I had to give one brief after-dinner talk, eat one more meal of rubber chicken slathered in mystery sauce, sleep one more night with my head on a lumpy pillow. I was ready to return to my wife and the comforts of home.

During this tour, my fortieth birthday had come and gone, a statistic that pleased me only when I considered the alternatives. In its passing, my thirty-ninth year seemed to have taken a most precious asset along with it, namely, my sense of humor about getting older. I was supposed to talk to nearly a thousand people about "The Power and Joy of Aging" in just a few hours, and I was feeling more than a little hypocritical.

The phone rang.

I answered quickly, hoping it would be Roma. Instead, I heard the voice of the gentleman who was to introduce me at the evening presentation.

"Great news, Mr. Metcalf," he said. "A woman by the name of Sylvie Washington was at your seminar yesterday. She enjoyed it so much that she wants to introduce you tonight."

"I'm flattered."

"But the best part is, she's 101 years old."

How could being 101 years old be the best part of *anything*, I wondered?

"Everyone here respects Sylvie," my host continued. "It's really something of an honor that she's asked to introduce you. She's never done that before."

"Gosh, that's wonderful," I said, forcing a grin. "Gee, imagine that, 101."

"I knew you'd be pleased," my caller said.

Everything Old Is New Again

That evening, as I sat at the head banquet table going over the presentation notes, my host tried to point out Sylvie. All I could see, several tables away, was the top of a snow-white, closely cropped head of thick, tightly curled hair.

A few moments later, the president of the organization took his place at the podium and introduced Sylvie. I glanced up. This time my view was blocked by the group's sudden, standing ovation for the woman who approached the stage.

It was not a good sign for the speaker, I thought, that this woman was getting a standing ovation *before* she began to talk. I was uneasy, but it didn't make sense: how could I possibly feel threatened by a 101-year-old woman?

I was about to find out.

I finally caught sight of her. A man was helping Sylvie up the stairs and across the stage. She moved slowly but casually, as though she had long ago adjusted to her tiny, shuffling gait. Her body stooped from a curvature of the spine that made her appear about a foot less than her already diminutive five-foot frame. Her silver hair shone in the backlighting, which also cast a glow on her light-chocolate skin. She wore gold-rimmed glasses that made her eyes seem unnaturally large and bright.

She appeared fairly healthy, but Sylvie's attire hinted at eccentricity. She wore high-top tennis shoes and four strands of heavy African trade beads that looked as if they weighed at least ten pounds. Her dress looked like a Rorschach test designed by Barnum and Bailey.

But for all the drama and visual interest, the first thing that struck me was her grin. It was a grin, not a smile—an expression with more natural humor and life than any I had seen.

Sylvie was so short that when she stepped behind the podium she nearly disappeared. I could just see her pale hair. Then a thin arm shot up and a long-fingered, delicate hand waved frantically. That cracked everyone up. She got a huge laugh and even more applause.

A twinge of nervousness and, *yes,* jealousy, tweaked my stomach lining—or, was it the rubber chicken with *sauce la strange* dinner?

As the laughter died down, a resourceful hotel employee rushed a short set of steps on stage and Sylvie's brown-eyed, gold-spectacled, grinning face appeared above the dais. "I've never talked to a group this large before," she said. Her voice was strong and vital. "I guess, after a hundred and one years, it's about time?"

More laughter. I was starting to understand at least one reason this woman made me uncomfortable: she was funnier than I was!

"I heard Mr. Metcalf speak yesterday," she said, nodding in my direction. "He did an eight-hour workshop. Imagine? Eight hours. That's the longest I've been awake at one stretch in better than twenty years."

I joined in the laughter. But I felt even more nervous. Not just because she was funny; it was something else I couldn't quite name.

"I've got a lot of respect for that man," Sylvie continued. "He said things the other day that I've been trying to tell my friends for the best part of a hundred years. I *do* those things he talks about. Been doing them for a long time. I believe the humor skills he told you about are a big part of why I'm here. And, my life hasn't been a joyride, either."

Then she told her life story—just the major high and low points, thank God, or we would probably still be there. My nerves quieted as I listened.

Born in Alabama in 1884 to a large farming family, Sylvie was the eldest of seven children. Her mother, Sarah Epsteine, had come South from New York to help establish schools for black children who had been orphaned by the Civil War. Sarah had been "met harshly by some Southerners who didn't understand her mission, and befriended by a few of the locals who donated a barn for her first school."

Sylvie's father, Axel Framer, was an ex-slave who had carved out a modest and barely profitable farm on land that his former owner had allowed him to purchase in exchange for ten years of labor. Axel wanted to read and write, and so he showed up in Sarah's first class along with about two dozen other students ranging in age from seven to seventy.

Axel and Sarah married. Sylvie was their third child, but the first to live past three months of age. Black and white, Christian and Jew, Sylvie Washington grew up being hated by nearly everyone who wasn't a member of her immediate family. The rest of her story was equally remarkable.

The balance of her history included an education in New York, marriage to a famed vaudeville musician, giving birth to five children—three of whom died before age seven, several years living in France, then two years in a Nazi concentration camp, and the death of her husband. There was more, much of it just as numbingly tragic.

The audience was in tears, and Sylvie had covered the entire century in less than ten minutes. Great introduction for a humor talk, I thought, wiping my eyes and praying that Sylvie would just go on, and they would all forget about me.

"So, how come I'm still smiling?" Sylvie asked her teary-eyed audience. "I'll tell you why. Because I've been doing those humor thingamajigs that C.W. Metcalf told us about all my life, that's why. But you know what really gets to me?" She paused for a moment, surveying them. "They paid Mr. Metcalf a lot of money to tell you about those humor skills. Heck, if you'd asked me, I could have told you over coffee for free!"

A roar of laughter and more applause.

Then Sylvie looked at me and grinned. Leaning slightly toward my table, she blurted out, "Got'cha!" And broke into a whooping laugh that sounded like a cross between an insane crow and a backfiring diesel engine. The audience laughed even more raucously, and so did I. Sylvie then motioned me up to the stage. I rose and walked forward to begin a speech that I knew would be very anticlimactic.

I was grateful that before I reached the stairs leading up to the stage, an audience member asked Sylvie a question.

"Sylvie, did you ever remarry?"

"Not until about three years ago," she replied, and asked her young husband of eighty-four to stand and be recognized. I noticed he was as big as she was small. Completely bald and grinning hugely, he waved at the crowd. More applause.

Oh, Lord, I thought, there's been more applause in this introduction than I could expect in an entire sixty-minute speech. Save me, I pleaded silently, please. I can't do this. I was now standing near Sylvie and slightly behind her.

"You know what?" she asked of the audience. "My husband's seventeen years younger than I am. His favorite joke is to roll over in the morning, wake me up with a little nudge in the ribs and say, 'Honey, you know, you're old enough to be my mother.' "

More laughter. I felt as if I might be disappearing, which would have been nice.

"Sylvie?" Another person in the audience queried. "I work in a nursing home. And, this is hard to ask but, I was wondering if, well, if you and your husband still . . . that is . . . are you, uh, physically active in an intimate way?"

Sylvie whooped that laugh and said, "Dear, if you're asking a woman my age for advice about sex, you're in big trouble."

Uh huh . . . Laughter. Was I invisible yet?

"Tell you the truth," Sylvie said, leaning forward to rest her elbows on the podium, "we still have sex. That is, we started to when we got married, but we haven't finished yet."

Hilarity rocked the room. I took advantage of this to tug on Sylvie's sleeve. She smiled at me. I covered the microphone and whispered.

"You're wonderful. The best speaker I've ever heard. Why don't you just tell them what you have to say, and I'll listen. Later, I'll donate my speaking fee to the organization. I just can't follow you. You're too good."

Sylvie beamed. I was off the hook. She held my hand. But her grip did not seem to indicate that she was ready for me to leave.

The audience finally calmed down. Then, Sylvie spoke: "Mr. Metcalf said the sweetest thing, just now."

I cringed.

"He said that I was such a wonderful speaker that he didn't want to follow me. Well, I'm flattered, because I've heard him, and he's good. But, so he won't be uncomfortable, I've got a plan. I'll let him speak right now, then I'll finish the introduction. That way he won't have to follow me."

She stepped back and led the applause. I was on.

I've spoken after CEOs, international dignitaries, and major and minor luminaries, and never felt intimidated until that moment. I decided to start my talk by telling the truth. What the heck, a guy has to take a risk now and then.

In my opening statement I explained my terror at having to follow Sylvie, and the reason for it. I'd been traveling around the world for years, telling people that they ought to develop humor skills. And yet, that very day I had been in a rotten mood. Sylvie threatened me because—against far worse difficulties than I had ever faced—she had become what I wanted to be. She was completely unpretentious, just who she was, and everyone who heard her felt blessed by her humor. Listening to her had made me feel like a charlatan.

I concluded by saying that I hoped one day to have the understanding of humor that life had granted her.

I stayed in touch with Sylvie until she died at age 103. Whenever I needed a reminder of the value of humor, I'd give her a call, or, coincidentally, one of her rambling letters would show up in my mailbox. (She dictated those letters to a secretary, and sometimes got a bit carried away.) I kept a journal of her comments, observations, and asides that is now in my Humor Annex. Every year, her words in that journal make more sense; especially an entry from her last letter to me.

"Being old isn't just bad or just good, it isn't just sad or just funny," she wrote. "Truth is that being older is similar to the rest of your life; some of it is Heaven on earth, and then there's the plain old Mondays."

Boomer Bummer—Help, I'm a Groan-Up

Just as the kids at the Center for Attitudinal Healing eased my fear of death and sickness, Sylvie lessened my terror of growing old and seemed to elevate the process to an art. She set a living example of what growing older *could* be like if one did what she referred to as those "humor thingamajigs" (humor skills). She wasn't just aging gracefully, she was having fun.

But perhaps the larger question is why so many baby boomers are obsessed by encroaching *middle age*. After all, my parents and grandparents avoided declaring a state of national emergency when they turned forty. They, like most survivors of the Great Depression, accepted middle age and welcomed its companion, economic security.

In contrast to them, my boomer friends and I are pained by having become the people *we never trusted*. No kidding. In the sixties we were advised by *our* heroes never to trust anyone over thirty. As teens, Roma and I saw a movie called *Wild in the Streets*. The hero, a young rock and roller, runs for president, wins, and consigns all middle-aged adults to "camps," where they are forced to take LSD. (For younger readers—this did not actually happen.)

For years, advertising was geared toward flattering *us*—the biggest, richest younger generation in history. Television, radio, and the print media hinted that if we spent enough money on the right stuff, we would be—as in the Bob Dylan song—*forever young*.

Most boomers I know were irritated by turning thirty something, but FORTY? Ye gads. Forty is the minimum age set for legal protection in cases of age discrimination. Forty is too old to be drafted in a national emergency. Forty is what your parents were. Forty is middle-aged.

No!
Yes.

As my wife and I enter the early stages of preparation for Camp Antiquity (ha, ha, ha), we, and quite a few others in our age group, have begun to complain about aches and pains that we were never supposed to have. Staying up all night has become impossible, and both of us have noticed of late that ninth-graders are allowed to pilot commercial jets and become doctors. (I distinctly remember my father complaining about the same thing in the 1950s.) It means that because it's less troubling, we are inclined to *see* young people as younger than their chronological years, rather than to see ourselves growing old.

I'm not personally offended by those **If it's too loud, you're too old** T-shirts; in fact, I wish I'd owned one back when Jimi Hendrix was playing "The Star Spangled Banner." But I dread the day when someone gives me a shirt like the one Sylvie's great-grandson gave her. On the front were the words, **I Love the Music!** On the back, the shirt proclaimed, **I'm Deaf!** She wore it whenever she stuffed plugs in her ears and visited the bar where the boy played in a heavy-metal band.

Something's Happening Here

The ads for face cream and exercise equipment may have promised the baby boomers perpetual youth, but the ads, like so many politicians in recent years, were apparently *lying*. Although I will never condemn those who work at maintaining good looks, high energy and health, I believe the boomers need to spend as much time on *building good character* as they do on restoring their waistlines or working toward the perfect marathon time.

If we don't learn to accept (I didn't say *like,* I said *accept)* the inevitability of growing older, we are going to suffer—and there will be a lot of us *to suffer.*

Between the years 1776 and 1986, the average life expectancy in the United States more than doubled, from thirty-five to seventy-five. From 1990 through the year 2000, the fifty- to sixty-four-year-old bracket will grow by 25 percent, but the number of Americans under fifty will increase only 3.5 percent. For a clearer understanding of how significant these changes are, you need to realize that more than half the people to reach age sixty-five in all human history are alive right now!

Many insist that the problems associated with aging, including the so-called generation gap, have been with us throughout history. But statistics show a vital difference between history and the present. Only in the past fifty years has any significant percentage of the population lived long enough to create the social challenges of aging that we face today.

The generation gap was easier to hop across in 1776. By age fifteen, young women were married and having babies, and young men had already spent one third of their lives apprenticing in a career. Most people died by age thirty-five. By 1996, the generation gap will reach from eighteen to seventy-eight—a forty-year increase.

Until recently we, as members of society, have viewed aging as a personal and family issue—a curiosity, not a trend. The boomers will be the first body of humanity to confront the issue *en masse.*

Frankly, that worries me.

Never Trust Anyone Under Thirty!

Everyone needs a teacher, a family member, or a friend—someone like Sylvie, who *proves* that it is possible to experience fun, in addition to aches and pains, in the elder years. How are today's young people supposed to gain a positive attitude toward age when they see their forty-year-old parents *freaking out* upon discovering a few gray hairs? Concern about one's appearance is great, but obsessive fear is not.

In a society where no one wants to grow up, we have a problem that far outstrips the similarities and differences between Janis Joplin and Sinead O'Conner, Elvis Presley and M.C. Hammer, the Beatles and Guns 'n' Roses.

The Illusion

Obsessive vanity is often the first symptom of our fear of aging; very few of us find the humor in not having the flat tummies, firm fannies, flawless skin, and golden waves of hair that Madison Avenue has raised to the status of cultural icons. There's a whole new market for muscle cars, health spas, plastic surgery, and low-impact aerobics classes.

I've already admitted that I spent time writing ad copy (we all have a few spiritual lapses), an experience leading me to speculate that the "art" of advertising lies partially in piquing fears and manipulating weaknesses. As we boomers tumble toward middle age, however, the idea that youth is desirable and aging is not has finally started to change—thanks to a few smart media people.

Consider *Lear's* magazine. For years, women who were interested in fashion had to see it modeled by twenty-year-old women. It's one thing to be forty, trying to become the best-looking forty-year-old you can. But it's a cruel joke to suggest that forty-year-olds can be beautiful only if they manage to look twenty. With impossible goals, women are doomed to discontent. (Yes, you can have plastic surgery, but no matter how much surgery you have, there's still going to be a difference between you and someone twenty years younger.)

When Frances Lear started *Lear's,* geared originally to the woman who "wasn't born yesterday," the pundits of publishing predicted that it would flop. Instead, it became a raging success, indicating that many of us would be willing to look for the advantages of increasing years if we had greater opportunities to do so.

A similar trend toward acceptance seems to be reaching *Esquire* magazine and *GQ,* where I was gratified to see balding male models come into vogue. (By the looks of these guys, though, I suspect they are twenty-eight-year-olds who just shaved their heads to get a job.)

Do such signs indicate a more enlightened attitude? In some cases, yes; at least, my wife thinks so. (Frances Lear is one of Roma's humor heroes.)

But generally speaking, such changes refer to the vast buying power of the boomer age group. Recent polls indicate that most people in North America today consider thirty to be the ideal age, not twenty-one as a few decades ago.

Trust me, the marketing and promotion people are at work, and they don't miss a beat. Soon the perfect age will be forty. In fact, I wish the ad folks would get on with it. I need to start feeling happier about my middle age, and kids of today need role models that they can contradict now, and emulate in twenty years.

Another Brick in the Wall

Sixties youths excelled at being terminally serious in criticizing the over-the-hill crowd; and, heaven knows, *a few* of today's teens and young adults are doing their best to seem equally nasty. You may have seen the bumper sticker that appeared a few years ago: **DIE, YUPPIE SCUM!** (It gave me a warm, fuzzy feeling about postboomers' esteem for their elders.) And I was heartened by the bicoastal fad that had young people wearing black-on-black clothing. (Were they preparing for a funeral? Was it mine, I wondered?)

Then my boomer friends in their thirties and forties co-opted the all-black style and another hallmark of youth was gone. Sure, we've given them our music. The young are as apt to listen to Mick Jagger, Grace Slick, David Bowie, Tina Turner, and Paul McCartney, who are middle-aged, as they are to play Bon Jovi or Paula Abdul. Although rock and roll, or some semblance thereof, provides a strand of musical understanding between younger people and me, I think we're teaching kids more about paranoia and narcissism than the values that can make the real difference between being alive and having a life.

Because we boomers will literally own the country and, for the first time in history, outnumber young members of society, we have a special obligation to avoid denying the younger generation its rights. We need to demonstrate the strengths of age by cultivating a truly broad perspective and real understanding of life's value. If we don't, we may become the targets of enormous envy and eventual rage.

As the most highly populated generation of all time, we have the opportunity to cope with aging in such a way as to change its meaning from negative to positive. We might use our influence to bring about vast social changes in everything from ecological suicide and racism to poverty and world hunger.

Whatever we might accomplish, however, we must first know how to laugh, love, and live with ourselves and our fears.

What, Me Worry?

If you're lucky, aging is a reality you will have to deal with. Humor skill development can help us to honor and cope with our fears so that we can draw the best from our aging.

In the past, commentary on the subject has been offered either in professional journals, which habitually bemoan the trials of growing old, or in the popular press, with its ceaseless jabbering about what great fun the *golden years* will provide. Some very real causes for the fear of aging make it important to separate our fantasies from legitimate worries.

Only a few decades back, *old* meant chronological age. Now we have a growing population of people who just won't fit that mold, no matter how hard we try to stuff them into it. The label most frequently applied to them is *Young-Old,* to distinguish them from the *Old-Old.*

Young-Old might describe people from age 55 to 105, because it includes elders who are healthy, financially stable, active members of one community or another, involved politically and socially, and having a pretty good time. People like Pearl Miller, known to her swimming companions at Senior Olympic games as "Coach."

"Why do I swim?" she asks. "Because it keeps me healthy and mentally alert. I jump in the water with young men the first thing every morning." As I write this, Coach is still swimming every day at age ninety-three.

Another of the Young-Old is Jim Law, an African-American who at age sixty-two, after a career as a college psychology professor and administrator, entered his first Senior Olympic contest "as a lark." He had taken numerous precautions—a physical exam that led him to adopt a macrobiotic meal plan and regular exercise to lower his high cholesterol. During a competition in fall 1990, Jim won all three races he entered and set national records in every one.

Although it is true that moderate exercise has been shown to slightly reverse biological aging in some people, most sports psychologists say that light aerobic and free-weight exercise only three times a week, combined with proper diet and vigorous social interaction, is plenty for most of us.

Which brings me to my boomer friends who are exercise freaks seeking perfect physical condition as a defense against aging.

Don't I Look Marvelous?

Many of my friends are exercising more and eating better today, in hopes of a healthier tomorrow, and I think that's wise. Such practices may extend life, and can certainly make living more enjoyable than it would otherwise be. You will nonetheless die one day. Exercising to combat fear of aging and death can be more damaging than helpful.

Obsessive, nonprofessional athletes suffer more injuries and experience more stress than their moderate counterparts. Overzealous exercise may shorten life by focusing us so narrowly on fitness that we withdraw from longevity-enhancing social and noncompetitive activities.

According to Dr. Rod Dishman of the University of Georgia's Behavioral Fitness Lab, the critical difference between obsessive-destructive and beneficial exercise appears to be **fun.** (Hey, there's that word again!) Evidently, in combination with a playful spirit, exercise is terrific no matter what your age as long as you're not overmedicating yourself (with painkillers and anti-inflammatory drugs) to cope with exercise-induced pain, and if you are not sacrificing your family, friends, and sense of fun to the fear of aging.

But focusing on physical exercise is only part of what keeps the Young-Old in that category. An essential element in longevity, according to eighty-five-year old author Ashley Montagu, is *neoteny*—juvenile characteristics carrying over into adulthood.

Recess

Ashley Montagu has written more than fifty books on subjects ranging from *The Natural Superiority of Women* to *The Nature of Human Aggression*. The secret of his long productive career, he says, is neotenous behavior. Montagu is convinced that emphasizing neoteny—childlike behavior—can help the rest of us live longer, healthier, more creative lives.

Notice the difference between *childish* and *childlike*. *Childish* refers to early, emergent personality traits such as selfishness and prolonged inappropriate, infantile behavior, such as whining, pouting, or throwing tantrums to achieve an end. *Childlike*, according to Montagu, means maintaining the neotenous qualities of childhood, including curiosity, openness, spontaneity, flexibility, creativity, playfulness, and joyfulness. If we do so, he contends, we will be physically and emotionally better for it.

Montagu's praise of neotenous behavior is supported by scientific studies as well as by anecdote. Studies from the Hannover Medical School in Germany showed that one neotenous trait—being outgoing and friendly—lowered cholesterol and uric acid and increased the activity of disease-fighting cells. James F. Fries, M.D., associate professor of medicine at Stanford University, writes that the human life span may well be dictated by genetic programming, but life-enhancing behaviors such as neoteny can add years to our lives. "You do those things throughout life," he says, "and it's like laying down good wine—you enjoy it twenty years from now."

My wife's parents are wonderful examples of the benefits bestowed by, among other things, neoteny. They are neither marathon runners nor competitive swimmers, but in their sixties they remain among the Young-Old by combining common sense with healthy neoteny:

1. A balanced low-fat, low-sugar, high-fiber diet.

2. Light exercise. (Although I'm sure they exercise in the dark, too.)

3. Constantly learning and adding to their store of information, new ideas, new experiences, even new friends, while honoring and cherishing the positive memories and old friends.

4. Laughter and play, and a lot of it. They are forever hauling Roma and me off to plays, movies, or the zoo. I find myself inspired by their effort to maintain their curiosity, wonder, and playfulness.

Then What's Old-Old?

The label *Old-Old* is now used to refer to deteriorating mental or physical health that severely limits an elder's daily activities. As we age, however, humor skills and neotenous behavior may well help defend us against feeling Old-Old. In a 1989 report, Dr. Dean Ornish at the University of California, San Francisco, showed that cardiac patients who were encouraged to activate their childlike imagination, and visualize their bodies as battling the heart-disease enemy, achieved the first documented reversal of arterial plaque buildup.

Despite continued discoveries in medical technology, the time may come when at least some of us will have to rely on care given by others. Some of us will experience the pain of Alzheimer's, cancer, blindness, deafness, and a multitude of other difficulties that afflict the body. Joan Borysenko points out that "Everybody dies of *something*."

Developing humor skills may not avert such problems, but they will at least enhance the time and health we do have. Further, the fluidity and flexibility of *umor* can make even a difficult journey easier to bear.

Who's in Charge Here?

As Sylvie eloquently stated, "Aging is sometimes a process of maintaining your balance while losing your control." Her point was that for many elders, the uncertainties of aging are its greatest trial, and a decreasing sense of control is the most stressful reality we face in getting older.

"Not knowing what's going to happen from moment to moment," she said, "is a problem that I just didn't appreciate when I was, say, in my seventies or so. At least, in my seventies, I was in charge of when I had to pee, for gosh sakes! Now, I'm wearing diapers again." As I recall, Sylvie laughed uproariously before concluding, "If at some point you can't find the humor in it all, you're dead. Or you might as well be."

Control *is* crucial to maintaining health as we grow older. Some very significant research on issues of control, health, and longevity has been done by Judith Rodin, Ph.D., a psychologist at Yale University.

At one stage, Rodin's work was focused on nursing-home residents. In that study, elders who were given control over simple decisions—when to have visitors, when to turn the lights on or off in their rooms, what time they ate—showed stunning positive effects. Over an eighteen-month period, the mortality rate of the group with control was 50 percent less than that of the nursing-home residents without such control.

Other studies show that maintaining even limited control over any area of one's life can have the same and even greater effects on health, mortality, and general alertness.

In similar research conducted by psychologist Richard Schulz, Ph.D, of the University of Pittsburgh, an unexpected side effect of the study proved illuminating and sad. Nursing-home residents were given various amounts of control over visits they received from local college students. That control significantly increased the elders' happiness and health. (Predictability, at least in some aspect of their life, evidently was the key.) But two years after the study ended, it was found that the residents who had been given control that was subsequently taken away were doing worse psychologically than those who had never been given control in the first place. But even this loss can be offset. Every study of how the sense of control affects health and well-being has some consistent factors that can help us maintain strength and self-determination as we age.

For one thing, we can take control of the way we explain our problems. (Most experts feel that explanatory styles are learned and therefore can be unlearned and refocused.) Research has begun to show that people who blame themselves for their troubles, making self-deprecating statements such as, "It's my fault," or "I never do anything right," are more likely to become depressed and to have other health problems than those who respond without self-blame, using such lines as, "Well, those things happen," or, "Glad it wasn't any worse."

That's a critical point, considering two primary attributes of humor skills that we discussed in earlier chapters:

1. The sense of control gained by choosing to access absurdity in adversity.

2. Developed optimism, which manifests itself in a disciplined sense of joy at being alive.

In speaking to my generation, I suggest that it is far easier to learn humor skills *now* instead of later. If you doubt this, ask a few of your retired friends. You will probably find that humor skills are not automatically granted along with that gold watch and lovely walnut plaque.

If You Can't Think of Anything Absurd Enough to Laugh About, Read This . . .

Sixty-five. A magical number if ever there was one. At sixty-five years, according to the wisdom of commerce, it is time to retire. You might assume, as I did, that some underlying intelligence and reasoning went into selecting that age as the line of demarcation between work life and retirement. Wrong.

In the 1880s, when human life expectancy was about forty-five, Otto von Bismarck, the ruler of Germany, needed to select a retirement age for civil servants. Combining a rare mixture of intelligence and bureaucratic slyness, he chose age seventy, figuring correctly that not many would make it. The Reich would save money. After much bickering, however, the retirement age was lowered to sixty-five, because at least 1.5 percent of the German population lived that long.

Fair enough.

When the U.S. Social Security act was passed in the thirties, von Bismarck's age marker was chosen. (Life expectancy in this country at the time was 61.9.)

Using the same math that von Bismarck applied just over 100 years ago would raise the present retirement age to 117. (I hope Congress doesn't see this.) In other words, sixty-five and retirement go together as naturally as eighteen and adulthood, twenty-one and maturity, or two-year-olds and silence.

Another bit of retirement rot to resist is beautifully explained by Ched Smiley, who went back to school at age sixty, got a degree in gerontology and became director of the Palm Harbor Multipurpose Center in Florida. He's seventy-five as I write this and says he plans to retire at ninety—maybe.

"Makes me mad when I see one of those damn bumper stickers that says: *Let Me Tell You About My Grandchildren*," said Ched in a recent newspaper interview. "I'd like to run the old fool off the road. Then I'd tell him, 'I don't care about your ——— grandchildren. Tell me about **you**!' "

The three most dangerous words for older people, Smiley thinks, are *When I Was.*

I couldn't agree more. Unlike Mr. Smiley (thank God for that name—and, yes, it's real), I can't speak from the experience of old age; and yet, when I hear people talk more about how great life used to be instead of what they still intend to do, I suspect that they're in trouble.

Smiley had a terrific lesson for us all when he reprimanded one acquaintance for always discussing the way it used to be.

"I made him an offer," Smiley said. "A thousand dollars if he would let me paint the windshield of his car black. Then he would go out on the highway and drive straight ahead for one mile, with only his rearview mirror to see from."

When the man declined, saying that he wasn't crazy, Smiley disagreed.

"Yes, you are crazy," Smiley told him. "Because you're going through life steering by your rear-view mirror."

Until I met Sylvie I had been doing something similar, even though I had just turned forty. I'd been speeding down the toll road of life (it sure isn't a FREEway) staring in the rear-view mirror, trying to go fast enough to escape getting older.

I hope the increasing awareness and political clout of aging boomers will lead to a more enlightened approach to elder care as well as promoting higher self-regard in that age group. I'll be out there working for it. Watch for me. I'll be the little bald guy with thick glasses and a T-shirt that reads **Don't Call an Ambulance: I'm Not Dead, I'm Just Slow**.

Dance on Their Graves

If you'd like some rules and tools for keeping a youthful spirit no matter how old you are, you might try following Montagu's suggestions, which I'll paraphrase.

- Reach out to the world by forming new acquaintances and by offering your time to help new and old friends alike.

- Give unconditional love even if you don't feel like it.

- Express joy and sorrow with laughter and tears. When children enjoy something, they laugh heartily. When they hurt, they cry. Repressing feelings and their expression leads to a loss of emotional depth.

- Play! Forget rules, game plans, points, and handicaps and just have some good silly fun with no particular goal.

Don't worry about seeming childish. If someone gives you a hard time, I offer you one of Sylvie's best observations.

One day, while Sylvie was taking a walk with her second husband and "one of his young friends in his eighties," they came to a halt while waiting for a traffic light to change. Sylvie started to do a little jig. She jigged a lot. She loved to dance. She would much rather dance than stand still—anytime. Her husband, accustomed to this behavior, took no notice.

But her husband's friend said, "For God's sake, Sylvie, act your age."

Sylvie told me that she stopped, "looked the old buzzard right in the eye, and said, 'You better be careful Herbert, I've buried everyone who ever told me that.'"

> *The best thing you can do for me after I've*
> *died is to shout my name every time you're*
> *happy.*
>> *—Celine, age fifteen*

12. Humor, Life,
and Death

Lend Me Your Fears

Death and dying create more anxiety than most topics; at the same time they generate a lot of comedy
as a defense. The boundary between grotesque and
sublime in dealing with death is difficult to define.
Most of us can probably identify with Woody Allen's
statement: "Death doesn't frighten me. I just don't
want to be there when it happens."

As with all forms of humor, varying cultural, familial, and personal perspectives make a remark that is
offensive to one terrifically funny to another. If you
have recently suffered the death of somebody you
cared for, or are still grieving over a long-ago loss,
much of the material in this chapter may seem, if not
offensive, at least inappropriate. But I intend only
to offer the lessons drawn from my experience—including years as a hospice trainer and volunteer—to
explain how humor skills have helped me move into,

through, and beyond grieving so that the living may celebrate in the light, instead of living in fear of the darkness.

Maybe It's a Plot

I certainly understand why many people fear aging—after *old* comes *dead*. (And that's all she wrote. Right?) But, if *old* is truly the stage before death, then poet Dylan Thomas was old at thirty-nine, Sylvie Washington was *not old* at ninety, and I've already *been old* at least a dozen times.

I wish death didn't frighten me. It does. So too does the potential pain. I don't want to die. And, if I must, I would like to die quietly, in my sleep, and wake up dead and quite surprised, thank you. I am in complete agreement with baseball great Leo Durocher, who said, at age eighty-nine: "I don't want to achieve immortality by being inducted into baseball's Hall of Fame. I want to achieve immortality by not dying."

Whenever my death does arrive, I hope to have shed my fear of it. I want to die as my ancestors prescribed in the ancient book of Norse poems called *The Elder Edda*. To die valiantly, whether in bed or on the battlefield, Vikings were instructed to exhale their last breath willingly, with joy in their hearts, because they were entering Valhalla, the Great Sky Hall of the Gods. I am fond of that idea because, no matter what one believes about life's postscript, dying valiantly is a worthy goal. To breathe out that one last breath without regret, with thanks, is a true consecration of life.

Tools for Life

To help myself and others—mostly to help myself—attain that ancient goal, I here submit to you my experiences with the people who taught me rules for living life as a profound pun, a lasting limerick, a sacred act of silliness.

Tool 1: A Perspective for Living

Like most people, I occasionally suffer from a case of *wish I had*s.

I wish I had:

- Forgiven Dad sooner, so that I could have been there when he died.
- Lightened up earlier.
- Known my grandmother better.
- Sobered up earlier.
- Attended Aunt Marge's funeral.
- Not been so selfish and cruel in so many relationships.
- Known, at the time, what Ed, my first hospice client, was trying to tell me.

At the same time that death reminds us of the *wish I had*s in our lives, it gives us an opportunity to change. By amending our wrongs and ridding ourselves of guilt, happiness becomes possible in the time that we have. Or, in the words of philosopher George Santayana, "There is no cure for life and death, save to enjoy the interval."

Those mistakes I am unable to amend by direct action add to my gratitude for not being condemned to repeat them—not too often, anyway. Well-l-l-l, more often than

I'd like. Okay, the truth is that these days I'm repeating a better class of mistakes.

My hospice client, Ed, who told me that I depressed him, is no longer a weight upon my conscience. Rather, he is a reference point for life, a North Star by which I guide my attitude toward death, and stay the course that includes humor, joy, and laughter.

Ed reminds me of the difference between selfishness that is disguised as caring, and true awareness that, only by giving freely of what I have been given, can I maintain the gift. I have made my amends to Ed in two ways.

First, I made a pilgrimage to his grave site several years after I'd gotten sober.

"God only knows what's blocking you up," he had said to me so long ago. Then he added: *"When you get it figured out, come back and visit me."*

And so I did. I returned to thank him, and to let him know that I had been released from at least a few major hindrances. I thought I would cry at the cemetery, but I laughed! There were no tears in me for Ed, only a quiet celebration of his honesty, his silly Disney pajamas, and the Goofy-emblazoned shirt he had left to me.

I completed the second part of my amends when, in return for his bequest, I placed a photograph of Sylvie Washington on his grave. I thought they should get to know each other.

So Long. It's Been Good to Know . . . Well, Most of You, Anyhow

When the letter from Sylvie arrived in the mailbox it had that heavy, linen feel to it, and it was square. Sure enough, as I opened it, a smaller envelope and folded card fell out. I opened the card. A photo of Sylvie's smiling face grinned out at me from the left side of the card. On the right-hand side, in plain script, it read:

My Last Going Away Party!
(Show up even if you didn't like me. I'm dead,
and I won't notice.)
—Love, Sylvie

On the same page were listed a day, an hour, an address where the funeral of Sylvie Washington would be played out, requests for an RSVP, and directions for contributing to a memorial fund for a youth-development program in Alabama.

It's hard to be stunned when a 103-year-old person dies. It is not as though her life and love were too brief. Typical of Ms. Washington, she'd left behind a funeral invitation that made me smile. It didn't assuage the guilt. A friend had died, a friend whom I had promised so many times that I would come to visit in the Northern Rockies, but. . . . Well, it was time. It was past time.

The funeral was a hybrid of music festival (some of the finest blues and jazz I'd ever heard), culinary contest (the kitchen overflowed with casseroles, chicken, and Sylvie's exotic favorite dishes), and wake (there was crying, there was laughter, there were maudlin eulogies and bawdy stories, a few arguments, one fight, a pledge of marriage, and an announcement of pregnancy—happily, from different couples). It was one fine party.

More than 300 people attended, most of them third- or even fourth-generation friends, Sylvie having outlived the original batch. I met her children, her grandchildren, her great, great, and so on, children.

Her great-grandson, the heavy-metal musician, opened the service with a song he'd written. He sang solo—and beautifully—strumming on an acoustic guitar.

Sylvie was laid out in a closed casket because she had not found an undertaker who could leave her smiling. She had opted, instead, for a larger version of the same grinning photo that had graced the invitation; it was on an easel in front of the casket.

I was flattered when Mr. Washington showed me the three photographs that hung in the bedroom, overlooking what had been the couple's bed: Mr. and Mrs. Washington doing the finest duet American Bat Face I've yet seen; a faded photo of her shaking hands with W. E. B. DuBois, and another of Sylvie holding the male and female twins who were her great-great grandchildren. The caption read: *Sarah and Axel at 3 mo., learning to laugh with Sylvie.*

And, a Child . . .

My first lessons in living with and learning from death came from the care and guidance of Jerry Jampolsky, his staff, and the children and families of the Center for Attitudinal Healing—so many lessons they would fill several volumes. One was a young girl named Shelly. She was thirteen, dying of a rare bloodborne cancer. She was so thin she seemed opaque in her wispy and white-skinned body, draped in a white gown as she appeared to float above the hospital bed. I stood with her parents and her older teen-age sister. We looked down at her. She was still breathing, but the oxygen entered and left her body with increasing effort.

Abruptly, her eyes opened wide and a shock wave of astonishment went through us all. She had not been conscious for several days, and the only sounds that had escaped her lips were low groans and murmurs.

"Someone's at the door," she said quite distinctly.

We all looked toward the door. Nothing.

Her mother moved closer and placed a hand on her child's arm.

"Where, honey?" she asked her daughter.

The child pointed straight up at the ceiling and smiled. Instinctively, we all glanced up. When our gaze returned to Shelly's face, her struggle with breathing was finished, and the smile faded very, very slowly.

I learned another lesson from a boy named Donny. Every morning when he got out of bed, the nine-year-old picked up the darts and stepped to a yellow line drawn on the floor. The line was exactly eleven feet from the dartboards that hung on his bedroom wall. His dad had made the targets for him. The rings were numbered from 1,000 to 1,000,000,000, and were carved into large, free-form cellular shapes. They represented the cancer cells that were multiplying in Donny's blood. Each dart was labeled *Healthy Cells.*

The little boy would take careful aim and then toss the darts, "killing" millions of invasive, sick cells every day. That exercise in control was often followed by more rounds of doctor checkups and various other treatments.

That was five years ago. Donny is fourteen now, and has been in remission from leukemia for three years. He still tosses a few darts at the board every morning, "for good luck," and he still visits the doctor, but not as often.

"Who knows?" Donny says, philosophically. "Maybe the game helped my mind know what I needed to do. For all I know, cancer cells don't like darts, and they got, uh, bored to death?"

For Harvey Brenner and the Buddha

> How to tell if your life on earth is through?
> If you're alive, it isn't.
> —Richard Bach

Lighten Up has, in a way, a third collaborator. If Harvey Brenner had refused to join me on that first journey to the Center for Attitudinal Healing more than a decade ago, I would not be writing this book. Our experiences at Tiburon started a healing process in us both.

Harvey's commitment to writing was secured in that assignment, and he went on to realize his dream of making a living and a difference through his literary talents. (He did much better on the making a living part after I left Los Angeles in 1980, and we quit working together. He assured me there was no connection. But then, he also assured me that Ronald Reagan would never be elected president of the United States.)

From his experiences at the Center, Harvey drew the strength he needed to re-create his own life. At an age when most men are starting to lower their expectations to cope with life's disappointments, Harvey Brenner raised his awareness, his sights, and his mortgage payments. He lost a wife through a painful divorce, but met and married Lynn Greenberg, the love of his life.

In doing so, he had the opportunity to learn about having sons, for Lynn's two teenage boys became part of his new family. He was able to help his two daughters from an earlier marriage move into joyful adulthood. He built and reaffirmed stronger, more loving relationships with his brothers. His efforts, through committee work in the Writer's Guild of America, helped the long-ignored writers of "industrial films" (those made for promotion or training in corporations) to receive union wages and benefits for their work. His artistic and administrative contributions to several altruistic projects continue to make a difference in the lives of thousands of children around the world. Harvey achieved, in his own words, "every worthwhile dream a person can have."

In June 1988 he was diagnosed with metastasized colon cancer. Further investigation revealed that his liver and most of the surrounding tissues were also riddled with the disease. Expectancy for survival was almost zero.

Harvey was angry at first, then he did everything he could to alleviate the disease. After four months of combined traditional and Chinese medicine, intensive meditation, visualization, prayer, diet, exercise, biofeedback, and group involvement with the Wellness Community in Santa Monica, the doctors were astonished to find that Harvey was in complete remission. No trace of his cancer remained. Two months later, the disease returned with a vengeance.

When I called Harvey, he told me, "Either this cancer wasn't through making me appreciate life, or it's an offer from the universe to audition for my role as first Jewish saint of Buddhism." It turned out to be an audition.

As his condition worsened, he made preparations. He spoke to each member of his family, one at a time. "Okay," he told them, "I might be dying. I'm ready."

They discussed their fear, hope, love, and anger.

Harvey later told me, "I let them know that I was ready to die, but they had to be willing to let me go. Otherwise, I might have felt compelled to hang around too long and create a lot of unnecessary suffering."

A few weeks before Harvey became the first Jewish saint of Buddhism, I sat with him and watched the NBA semifinals on television in his room at home.

"I can't help it, Harvey," I admitted. "I can't shake the idea that it's not fair for you to be heading off this soon."

"Fair?" He laughed. "If the world was fair, would there be any attorneys? Would there be a Pasadena Freeway? Would agents get 10 percent?"

I shook my head; these mysteries were beyond me.

"Now, listen up, C.W.," he went on. "I'm a dying man, and I am prone to words of wisdom. Unfair is the word we use for human stupidity, things like racism. Or it's for pitiful things like the death of an infant. Unfair is a sign that announces the city limits of human intelligence and understanding, that's all. If I die, it won't be unfair; it may be expensive, but it won't be unfair. Do you get it?"

"I'm not sure," I said.

Harvey smiled. "My life, right now, is perfect. I'm more in love with Lynn, happier for my kids, more successful at my work than I ever thought possible.

This is a great time to die. Remember when you and I were driving around L.A. that 100-degree summer, in an unairconditioned, brokendown car, looking for our first writing job together? My marriage was failing. My kids were struggling and sad, and my friends thought I was nuts. Even I thought I was nuts. Now, *that* would have been a rotten time to die.

"Now? I'm still handsome, happy, and, except for this cancer thing, pretty healthy. This is not unfair. This is just dying. And I'm getting a chance to feel it, to know it, to deal with it. Sometimes I hate it. I'm scared, and I cry because it hurts. Along with being born, which I don't remember all that well, this is the only other life event that happens just once—I think. Maybe not. But it's the only time I've ever died in this life, and I get to really *be* with it. I'm going to stay with this until the pain is unbearable, or my suffering is making it hard on Lynn, because it's mine, this death, it's mine. And I will not let dying cheat me of my own death."

He paused and laid his head back on the pillow. "Of course," he said, "ask me tomorrow and I might think the whole idea stinks. It's complex, this dying stuff. I can tell you that."

In a later conversation, much closer to his final days on the planet, he asked for my opinion on several concerns he had. Because he planned on cremation, and would have no headstone, per se, he was considering something appropriate for a memorial plaque.

"I've been thinking about something profound," he said. "Something like, 'Now, THIS is a deadline.' "

I cringed. He gloated.

"What are you going to have done with the ashes?" I asked.

"I know I want most of them turned into the soil of the flower garden out back," he said, "so I can pop up every spring and say hi to Lynn. But I was just fooling around with some last-minute notes; what do you think of this idea?" He paused.

"Well?" I said.

"To my agent: You took a pound of flesh on every deal we cut, so here's 10 percent of my ashes. It's the last you'll never see of me. I'll write when I get work."

Harvey died of cancer on April 3, 1989. He went out clear and at peace with his family, his friends, and himself.

One of the last things he told me was, "Make something out of our work in Tiburon, understand? Finish that job, or I'll come back to haunt you. Do you have any idea how a Jewish ghost haunts? It's *horrible*. Don't let the Rainbow Gang fade."

Okay, it's not a movie, not yet, but it is a book. So, *please,* Harvey, quit putting gefilte fish in my underwear. You were right. It's *horrible*.

GRIEF is a long-term process that may take months or even years to complete. When Harvey died, there was that unique hurt, as though a psychic limb had been severed, and I was left deeply wounded; it will become less painful. It will heal. I suspect that Harvey's death will leave a wound similar to a small scar I have borne on my thigh for forty years, because I learned similar lessons from both those wounds.

The mark on my leg resulted from a fall I took on a fishing trip in 1952. I had followed my uncle down a steep, rocky descent that led to the stream. I was balancing a new fishing rod with both hands, imagining myself to be a circus high-wire walker, thousands of feet above the earth.

"Watch out!" my uncle shouted.

Too late. The wire snapped. I arced out over the boulders—gripping my new rod as though I expected it to become a rocket ship and carry me to safety. The first impact was painful. I shrieked. My final meeting with the ground put me face first in the gravel, my fishing rod still extended stiffly before me, as I plowed several feet to a stop.

"Stay still, Butchie," my Uncle said. It was the same firm tone of voice he used if he saw a rattlesnake on the trail. I turned to stone.

"Good. Now, scream."

I had no time to wonder what he meant before I saw that his hunting knife was out and the tip slipped under the flesh of my thigh. I obligingly screeched as loud as my little lungs would allow. According to my uncle's account, a six-inch sliver of stone had pierced the front of my thigh, rather like a needle drawing invisible thread.

Today, I look at that bright, twin-toothed scar on my thigh and I smile. I remember not the pain, but the sun, the leaves and water of precious stones, the drama of my fall, and the miraculous recovery from my uncle's surgery. I can still see the silver flash of every one of the twenty-two rainbow trout we caught and released, still smell the campfire smoke as we prepared my "keeper" brown trout for lunch, and still taste the singular flavor of that fish.

In the same way, Harvey's passing reminds me of the lessons I learned from that earlier wound.

First, I must cry out and release my grief for him so that I may heal.

Second, as time passes I must celebrate the good Harvey brought me in the same way that I invoke the magic and beauty of that fishing trip; and I will share my positive memories of Harvey Brenner. It is important to spend time talking to another human being about the good, the moments of laughter, friendship, and joy that life has given us. Until we celebrate and remember the good, we have not fully exorcised the pain.

Third, I will cherish Harvey's laughter, his curiosity, his absurd optimism in the face of tragedy and, most of all, the deep moments of trust and love that he showed me men can share.

Harvey joins my Grandmother MacDonald, Sylvie, and so many others. He sits with my uncle and my forgiven father, on the banks of the Trinity River that flows through my history. I will join them, and we will sit around the picnic table, our eyes watering from the campfire smoke, savoring the taste of trout, laughing to release our pain and ourselves. That is the wounded gift of Harvey's passing—a reminder of life, laughter, and lessons learned on our way to the river.

Until then, I will try to do as the Buddha instructed. When the great spiritual leader lay dying, his disciples asked for some last words to live by. It's recorded that he smiled and, with his last breath, said: "Do your best."

Epilogue:
Calling All Clowns

What changes has a humorous approach brought about in your life? (We're interested in *umor* belly-flops as well as perfect tens. Olympic Gold Medalist diver Greg Louganis learned as much about his sport by hitting his head on the board during Olympic competition as he had from every perfect dive he had made.)

Please write to tell us about humor used in your family, workplace, social life, and encounters with difficulty. Our address is:

C.W. Metcalf & Company
2801 S. Remington, Suite 2
Fort Collins, Colorado 80525

We look forward to hearing from you. Your advice may help others.

Notes

1. Lighten Up and Live, or Tighten Up and Leave

page 3 Stephan J. Corrie, *Cockpit Voice Recorder Group; Chairman's Factual Report of Investigation* (Washington, D.C.: National Transportation Safety Board, September 1, 1989).

page 3 Corrie, pp. 82–83. The voice-recorder transcript from United Flight 232 shows that not only Captain Haynes but other crew members used humor to handle their increasing tension as the jet approached the runway.

page 9 John Morreall, *Taking Laughter Seriously* (Albany: State University of New York, 1983), p. 108. Humor and flexibility are connected.

page 9 Edward de Bono's comments were made during his lecture at Boston '91, a university colloquium sponsored by the Young President's Organization, April 1991.

page 10 Daniel Goleman, "Humor Found to Aid Problem-Solving," *The New York Times,* 4 August 1987.

pages 10–12 Norman Cousins, *Head First: The Biology of Hope* (New York: E. P. Dutton, 1989), p. 138. Positive emotions enhance the benefits we gain from exercise.

page 12 Arthur Koestler, "Humour and Wit," *Encyclopaedia Britannica,* 1990 ed., p. 682. Laughter is the luxury reflex.

2. Learning It the Hard Way

page 19 *There Is a Rainbow Behind Every Dark Cloud* (19 Main Street, Tiburon, CA 94920: Center for Attitudinal Healing, 1978). For more information about the Center and its philosophy, see Gerald G. Jampolsky, *Love Is Letting Go of Fear* (New York: Bantam, 1979, 1981) and *Teach Only Love* (New York: Bantam, 1983).

page 22 *A Course in Miracles* (P.O. Box 635, Tiburon, CA 94920: Foundation for Inner Peace, 1975).

page 25 George Vaillant, *Adaptation to Life* (Boston: Little, Brown, 1977).

3. Dare to Be Foolish

pages 46–49 William W. Ruch, *Psychology and Life,* 7th ed. (Glenview, Ill.: Scott, Foresman, 1963, 1967), pp. 440–441. Selye and the general-adaptation syndrome.

pages 49–50 Joan Borysenko, *Minding the Body, Mending the Mind* (Reading, Mass.: Addison-Wesley, 1987), pp. 16–17. The need for power; immunity; the effects of negative mental imagery.

page 51 *Alcoholics Anonymous,* 3rd ed. (New York: Alcoholics Anonymous World Services, 1939, 1976), pp. 85–87. The alcoholic's need to meditate.

page 51 Norman Vincent Peale, *The Power of Positive Thinking* (New York: Fawcett Crest, 1952, 1956), pp. 186–187. Deep relaxation and emptying the mind.

page 53 Harry Kitano, "The Japanese Family in America," *Ethnic Families in America,* Charles Mindel et al., eds. (New York: Elsevier Science Publishers, 1988). Restraint in traditional Japanese families.

page 62 Koestler, "Humour and Wit," p. 684.

4. Escape from the Center of the Universe: The First Humor Skill

page 69 Corrie, *Cockpit Voice Recorder Group,* pp. 34–35.

5. Take Yourself Lightly and Your Work or Problem Seriously: The Second Humor Skill

pages 94–95 Nancy Benac, "U.S. getting fatter, won't admit it," for the Associated Press reprinted in *Oregonian,* 3 May 1991. Statistics on excessive weight and stress.

page 95 John Cleese, *Wall Street Journal,* 1 August 1988. Cleese refers to the same idea in this article, saying, "When you charge the enemy machine-gun post, don't waste energy trying to see the funny side of it. Act narrow-mindedly. But the moment the action is over, we need to return to the open mode—to open our minds again. . . . "

pages 95–96 Ruch, *Psychology and Life,* p. 441. Comments by psychologist S. J. Lachman after reviewing work on the general-adaptation syndrome.

page 96 Robert Ornstein and David Sobel, *Healthy Pleasures* (Reading, Mass.: Addison-Wesley, 1989), p. 278. Study of nursing homes by E. J. Langer and J. Rodin cited. For further information about the relation between stress and control, see Chapter 10, "The Optimism Antidote."

page 97 Alvin Toffler, *Future Shock*. (New York: Random House, 1970), p. 2. Future shock is here.

page 102 Gerald Coffee, *Beyond Survival: A POW's Inspiring Lesson in Living* (New York: Berkley Books, 1990), pp. 130–131.

page 103 Johanna Neuman, "Ex-hostages felt like 'blind rabbit in a box,'" *USA Today*, 2 August 1989, and Linda Dowlen, "Humor helped hostages cope," Fort Collins, Colo. *Coloradoan*, 10 June 1987.

pages 103–104 Comments pertaining to Tom Sutherland's release were made on various newscasts. Later, at a YPO University (January 25–30, 1992), Sutherland explained how humor had been important to his survival.

6. Misery and Pain Are Free, but Joy Has a Price: The Third Humor Skill

page 125 Ornstein and Sobel, *Healthy Pleasures*, pp. 153–154. Healthy and unhealthy forms of denial.

page 126 "Affirmative Reaction: The Power of Positive Thinking," *Vogue*, June 1988, p. 128.

page 127 Coffee, *Beyond Survival*, p. 125.

page 128 John Robinson, "I Love My TV," *American Demographics*, September 1990, pp. 24–25. Estimates vary depending on whether primary, secondary, and tertiary viewing are included, but one thing is certain: for many Americans, viewing television is *the* primary leisure activity. When only primary viewing is considered, television takes 40 percent of the average person's leisure time. Research shows that the more leisure you have, the more hours you spend in front of the set. Statistics show that between 1965 and 1975 people gained an average of five hours of free time a week, and spent all of it watching television.

page 138 John Cassidy and B.C. Rimbeaux, *Juggling for the Complete Klutz*. (Palo Alto, Calif.: Klutz Press, 1988).

page 139 Jane Sanborn, *A Bag of Tricks* (Search Publications, 1984. P.O. Box 167, Florissant, Colorado 80816). A book of noncompetitive games.

page 139 Matt Weinstein and Joel Goodman, *Everybody's Guide to Non-Competitive Play* (San Luis Obispo, Calif.: Impact Publishing, 1988).

page 144 Christian Hageseth III, M.D., *A Laughing Place* (Fort Collins, Colo.: Berwick Publishing, 1988), pp. 62–64. Hageseth discusses *gelastolalia.*

7. Humor: An Antidote for Terminal Professionalism

page 151 Jim Impoco, "Dying to Work," *U.S. News & World Report,* 18 March 1991, p. 24. Article about death from overwork.

page 152 *Wall Street Journal,* 26 April 1991. Chronic fatigue reported among Japanese.

page 152 *Wall Street Journal,* 12 August 1991. Long work hours in Japan.

page 152 Jeff Shear, "The Dream Out of Reach for Japanese," *Insight,* 3 September 1991, pp. 8–17. Detailed feature about life and work in Japan.

page 152 David E. Sanger, "Death by Overwork—Study of Japan Offices," *The New York Times,* reported in *San Francisco Chronicle,* 20 March 1990.

page 153 "Japan's Corporate Generals 'killed in action' by stress," *Denver Post,* 24 July 1987.

page 154 Yoshiaki Itoh, "Worked to Death in Japan," excerpted from the Tokyo financial weekly *Japan Economic Journal* in the March 1991 *World Press Review,* p. 50.

page 154 Cindy Skrzycki, "Overachievers on Brink of Burnout Are Seeing the Light, Lightening Up," *Washington Post,* reprinted in *Los Angeles Times,* 17 November 1989.

pages 154–155 *Wall Street Journal,* 7 May 1991. Insurance survey of 600 United States workers.

page 155 "Downsizing Record Set by Firms in Year; 56% Report Job Cuts," *Wall Street Journal,* 12 August 1991. Report on AMA statistics about downsizing.

pages 155–156 Jack Gordon, "Who Killed Corporate Loyalty?" *Training,* March 1990, pp. 25–32. Statistics cited from *Business Week.* Gordon's excellent article explores in depth the reasons for a so-called decaying work ethic.

page 158 Thomas Stewart, "Business Is Cracking the Whip," *Fortune,* October 1990, pp. 121–128.

page 160 Gabriella Stern, "As the Going Gets Tougher, More Bosses Are Getting Tough with Their Workers," *Wall Street Journal,* 18 June 1991. Pressure is on CEOs.

page 166 Daniel Goleman, "Humor Found to Aid Problem-Solving," *The New York Times,* 4 August 1987. Humor promotes creativity and effectiveness.

pages 167–168 Brian Moss, "Workaholics' Shiny Badge of Honor Losing Luster," *New York Daily News,* reprinted in *Coloradoan,* 8 September 1987. Robert Rosen's comments on workaholism versus hard work.

page 169 Bridget O'Brian, "Frequent Fliers Get Input on Hiring at Southwest," *Wall Street Journal,* 13 May 1991.

pages 170–171 "Whither the Work Ethic?" *Incentive,* August 1988.

8. Can't You Take a Joke? Etiquette for the Humor Impaired

page 173 Emily Post, *Etiquette: The Blue Book of Social Usage* (London and New York: Funk & Wagnalls Co., 1945), p. 43.

page 178 Charles Mindel et al., eds., *Ethnic Families in America* (New York: Elsevier Science Publishers, 1988). The need to belong is basic to the human condition.

page 178 Robert Hendrickson, *Encyclopedia of Word and Phrase Origins* (New York: Henry Holt, 1987), p. 170. Origin of the dozens.

page 178 Stephen O. Murray, "Ritual and Personal Insults in Stigmatized Subcultures," Reinhold Aman, ed., *Maledicta: The International Journal of Verbal Aggression* (Philadelphia: Running Press, 1987), pp. 118–137. An academic look at insult humor.

page 179 Nancy Datan, "The Last Minority: Humor, Old Age, Marginal Identity," Lucille Nahemow et al., eds., *Humor and Aging* (Orlando, Fla.: Academic Press, 1986), p. 164. Anti-Semitic humor and persecution of the Jews.

page 181 Arthur Koestler, "Humour and Wit," *Encyclopaedia Britannica,* 1990 ed., p. 686. Babies, trust, and tickling are discussed.

pages 181–182 Datan, "The Last Minority," p. 162. Children and teasing. Also humor and elders.

page 184 Robert Bly, *Iron John* (Reading, Mass.: Addison-Wesley, 1990), p. 32.

page 186 Nancy Gibbs, "Office Crimes," *Time,* Oct. 21, 1991, p. 64.

page 192 Judith Martin, *Miss Manners' Guide to Excruciatingly Correct Behavior* (New York: Warner Books, 1983), pp. 185–186.

9. Why Do They Call It Happy Hour? Humor and Substance Abuse

page 197 *Alcoholics Anonymous,* 3rd ed. (New York: Alcoholics Anonymous World Services, 1939, 1976), p. xxvi.

pages 197–198 Jean Kinney, M.S.W., and Gwen Leaton, *Understanding Alcohol* (New York: New American Library, 1982), p. 211. Alcoholics who are addicted to other drugs and the history of alcohol. For more information on alcoholics using drugs, see *AA Membership Survey* (New York: Alcoholics Anonymous World Services, 1987). According to a survey of 7,000 AA members in the United States and Canada, 38 percent were addicted to other drugs before they joined the program.

page 199 Aaron Lathem, *Crazy Sundays,* Donald Hall, ed., *The Oxford Book of American Literary Anecdotes* (New York: Oxford University Press, 1981), p. 261. Drinking behavior of Scott and Zelda Fitzgerald.

page 201 Dee Pennock, " 'Happy Hours' Often Have Unhappy Consequences," *Senior Spectrum,* June 1991, p. 17. Elders and alcohol.

pages 200–204 Gail Milgram, *The Facts About Drinking* (Mount Vernon, N.Y.: Consumers Union of the United States, 1990). Reasons for drinking and statistics on various aspects of alcoholism. For more about alcoholics and alcoholism, see George Vaillant, *The Natural History of Alcoholism: Causes, Patterns, and Paths to Recovery* (Cambridge: Harvard University Press, 1983).

page 204 George E. Vaillant, "The Alcohol-Dependent and Drug-Dependent Person," Armand M. Nicholi, Jr., M.D., ed., *The New Harvard Guide to Psychiatry* (Cambridge: Belknap Press of Harvard University, 1988), p. 701. Demographics of alcoholism. Alcoholics and defense mechanisms.

page 208 Lester Grinspoon, M.D., and James P. Bakalar, J.D., "Alcohol Abuse and Dependence," *Harvard Medical School Mental Health Review* (Boston: *Harvard Medical School Mental Health Letter,* 1990.)

pages 210–211 Vaillant, *New Harvard Guide to Psychiatry,* p. 707. Requirements for treatment of alcoholism. For more information on AA meetings, see *AA Membership Survey* (New York: Alcoholics Anonymous World Services, 1987). According to the 1986 survey, the number of groups worldwide was more than 85,000.

page 212 Peter M. Monti et al., *Treating Alcohol Dependence* (New York: Guilford Press, 1989). Living sober.

10. What's So Funny? The Absence of Humor

page 220 The *Lighten Up* quiz is a condensed version of many similar tests.

page 220 Marilyn Elias, "A test to tell if you've got more than the blues," *USA Today,* 5 October 1984. Dr. Zung on depression.

page 223 Robert Ornstein, and David Sobel, *Healthy Pleasures* (Reading, Mass.: Addison-Wesley, 1989), p. 190. The importance of self-complexity.

pages 224–225 Gerald Klerman, "Depression and Related Disorders of Mood," Armand M. Nicholi, ed., *New Harvard Guide to Psychiatry* (Cambridge: Belknap Press of Harvard University, 1988), pp. 310–311. Clinical illness versus normal mood fluctuations.

pages 225–226 Mark Gold, *The Good News About Depression* (New York: Bantam Books, 1988), pp. 275–297. Depression in women and the elderly.

page 226 Jan Larson, "Treating the Whole Worker at Westinghouse," *American Demographics,* June 1991, pp. 32–33.

page 226 William Styron, *Darkness Visible* (New York: Random house, 1990), p. 7. Quotation from book about the author's own experience with depression. See pp. 32–33 in *Darkness Visible.*

page 227 "The Nature and Causes of Depression—Part I," *Harvard Medical School Mental Health Letter,* Vol. 4, no. 88, January 1988, pp. 2–3. This feature provides a detailed look at the causes, costs, and symptoms of depression.

pages 228–229 Christian Hageseth, M.D., *A Laughing Place* (Fort Collins, Colo.: Berwick Publishing, 1988.) The author discusses the use of humor in psychotherapy.

page 231 Styron, *Darkness Visible,* p. 84.

11. Talkin' 'Bout My Generation: For Sylvie

pages 242–243 Foundation for Wellness, producer, "Work and Aging," *Healthy People/Healthy Business* (P.O. Box 9818, Newport Beach, CA 92660: Foundation for Wellness, 1988), pp. 1–9. Facts, figures, and implications of an aging society.

page 247 Bernice L. Neugarten and Dail A. Neugarten, "The Changing Meanings of Age," *Psychology Today,* May 1987, pp. 29–33. The difference between Young-Old and Old-Old.

page 247 Leslie Lindeman, "Beating Time," *Modern Maturity,* June–July, 1991, pp. 26–35. Elder athletes—Jim Law and Pearl Miller—tell what it takes.

page 248 Dishman. *See* William Sherman, Ph.D., "Running Your Body into the Ground," *Longevity,* September 1990, p. 33.

pages 248–249 Edwin Kiester, Jr., "The Case Against Growing Old," *Longevity,* September 1990, pp. 22–26.

page 250 Montague and Ornish. *See* Edwin Kiester, Jr., "The Case Against Growing Old," *Longevity,* September 1990, pp. 22–26.

page 250 Joan Borysenko made the comment at a lecture in Fort Collins, Colo., May 1989. She pointed out that "all the saints are dead, and they all died of something."

pages 251–252 Robert J. Trotter, "Regaining Control," *Longevity,* December 1989, pp. 62, 66. The loss of control compared to the lack of control.

page 253 Foundation for Wellness, "Work and Aging," pp. 1–9. The retirement concept.

Readings and Resources

To learn more about humor and related subjects discussed in *Lighten Up,* we suggest that you peruse one of the following books or tapes. If you don't like the one you've chosen, give it to somebody you don't like—and choose another! Far from being comprehensive, this selection of materials simply reflects our own taste. We have not included joke books, or the work of such great humorists as Will Rogers, Woody Allen, Dorothy Parker, and Herbert Hoover. But if you go to the library and look under Humor, Humorists, or Comedy, you are likely to find some stimulating material. Bookstore humor sections are also good places to begin exploring. And we encourage you to start a humor library of your own that includes anything from tapes to books, articles, and a list of personal "bloopers."

Alcoholics Anonymous. 3d ed. New York: Alcoholics Anonymous World Services, 1976. Alcoholism and Alcoholics Anonymous. This is the textbook of Alcoholics Anonymous and the progenitor of all 12-Step programs.

Alexander, Thomas, and Stella Chess. *Temperament and Development.* Larchmont, N.Y.: Brunner-Mazel, 1977. Humor and temperament.

Apte, Mahadev L. *Humor and Laugher: An Anthropological Approach.* Ithaca, N.Y.: Cornell University Press, 1985. Humor.

Benson, Herbert, M.D. *Your Maximum Mind.* New York: Random House, 1987. The mind–body connection.

Beveridge, William I. *Art of Scientific Investigation.* New York: Random House, 1960. Creativity.

Bly, Robert. *Iron John.* Reading Mass.: Addison-Wesley, 1990. Men and childhood teasing.

Borysenko, Joan. *Minding the Body, Mending the Mind.* Reading Mass.: Addison-Wesley, 1987. The mind–body connection.

Burns, David, M.D. *The Feeling Good Handbook.* New York: Morrow, 1989. The book offers a cognitive approach to overcoming problems, including the fear of foolishness, and provides readers with specific exercises.

Cannon, Walter B. *The Wisdom of the Body.* New York: Norton, 1963. The mind–body connection.

Cassidy, John, and B.C. Rimbeaux. *Juggling for the Complete Klutz.* Palo Alto, Calif.: Klutz Press, 1988.

Chopra, Deepak. *Creating Health: Beyond Prevention, Toward Perfection.* Boston: Houghton Mifflin, 1987. The mind–body connection.

Coffee, Gerald. *Beyond Survival: A POW's Inspiring Lesson in Living.* New York: Berkley Books, 1990. Surviving extreme stress—imprisonment.

Course in Miracles. P.O. Box 635, Tiburon, Calif. 94920: Foundation for Inner Peace, 1975. Attitudinal Healing.

Cousins, Norman. *Anatomy of an Illness as Perceived by the Patient: Reflections on Healing and Regeneration.* New York: Norton, 1979. The story of Cousin's recovery from illness, including the part humor played in his getting well.

———. *The Healing Heart: Antidotes to Pain and Helplessness.* New York: Norton, 1983. Surviving extreme stress—illness.

———. *Head First: The Biology of Hope.* New York: Dutton, 1989. The mind–body connection.

De Bono, Edward. *Lateral Thinking.* New York: Harper and Row, 1970. Creativity.

Dychtwald, Ken. *Bodymind.* New York: Jove Publishing, 1984. The mind–body connection.

Ellenbogen, Glenn C., ed. *The Directory of Humor Magazines and Humor Organizations in America.* New York: Wry-Bred Press, 1985.

Frankl, Viktor. *Man's Search for Meaning: An Introduction to Logotherapy.* New York: Simon and Schuster, 1959. Surviving extreme stress.

Freud, Sigmund. *Jokes and Their Relation to the Unconscious.* Translated by James Strachey. New York: Norton, 1960. Humor.

Fry, William F., Jr., M.D., and Waleed A. Salameh, eds. *Handbook of Humor and Psychotherapy: Advances in the Clinical Use of Humor.* Sarasota, Fla.: Pro Resource, 1987. Humor.

Gold, Mark. *The Good News about Depression.* New York: Bantam, 1988. Depression.

Goodman, Joel, ed. *Laughing Matters.* 110 Spring Street, Saratoga Springs, N.Y. 12866: The Humor Project. A quarterly magazine about humor available by subscription.

Hageseth, Christian III, M.D. *A Laughing Place.* Fort Collins, Colo.: Berwick Publishing Company, 1988. Humor and psychology, applications of humor techniques, plus the role of humor in psychotherapy.

Hansel, Tim. *You Gotta Keep Dancin'.* Elgin, Ill.: David C. Cook Publishing Company, 1985. Fighting despair and choosing joy, with a Christian emphasis.

Hutschnecker, Arnold A. *The Will to Live.* New York: Permabooks, 1951. Happiness.

Jampolsky, Gerald G. *Love Is Letting Go of Fear.* New York: Bantam, 1981. Attitudinal Healing.

———. *Teach Only Love: The Seven Principles of Attitudinal Healing.* New York: Bantam, 1983. Attitudinal Healing.

Kinney, Jean, and Gwen Leaton. *Understanding Alcohol.* New York: New American Library, 1982. Alcoholism.

Kushner, H. *When All You've Ever Wanted Isn't Enough: The Search for a Life That Matters.* New York: Summit, 1986. Happiness.

Kushner, Malcolm. *The Light Touch.* New York: Simon and Schuster, 1990. Humor.

McGhee, Paul E. *Humor: Its Origin and Development.* San Francisco: W. H. Freeman, 1979. Humor.

Metcalf, C.W. *Humor, Risk & Change.* Five audiotapes. Fort Collins, Colo.: C.W. Metcalf & Co., 1986. C.W. Metcalf's all-day humor workshop, plus the *Humor Allies.*

————. *Humaerobics.* Audiotape. Fort Collins, Colo.: C.W. Metcalf & Co., 1988. New humor exercises for body and mind set to music.

————. *Humor Allies.* Audiotape. Fort Collins, Colo.: C.W. Metcalf & Co., 1988. A collection of humor imagination exercises set to music.

————. *Humor, Risk & Change.* Videotapes. Des Moines: American Media, 1989. C.W. Metcalf's humor workshop: a training resource for organizations.

Milam, James, and Katherine Ketcham. *Under the Influence: A Guide to the Myths and Realities of Alcoholism.* Seattle: Madrona Publications, 1981. Alcoholism.

Milgram, Gail. *The Facts about Drinking.* Mount Vernon, N.Y.: Consumers Union, 1990. Alcoholism.

Millman, Dan. *Way of the Peaceful Warrior.* Tiburon, Calif.: H. J. Kramer, 1984. Happiness.

Mindess, Harvey, et al. *Antioch Humor Test: Making Sense of Humor.* New York: Avon, 1985. Humor.

Monti, Peter M., et al. *Treating Alcohol Dependence.* New York: Guilford Press, 1989. Alcoholism.

Moody, Raymond A., Jr. *Laugh After Laugh: The Healing Power of Humor.* Jacksonville, Fla.: Headwaters Press, 1978. Humor.

Morreall, J. *Taking Laughter Seriously.* Albany: State University of New York, 1983. Humor.

Nahemow, Lucille, McCluskey-Fawcett, and Paul McGhee, eds. *Humor and Aging.* Orlando, Fla.: Harcourt Brace Jovanovich, 1986. Humor.

The New Harvard Guide to Psychiatry. Cambridge, Mass. and London: Belknap Press of Harvard University Press, 1988. Chapters on alcoholism and depression.

Peale, Norman Vincent. *The Power of Positive Thinking.* New York: Fawcett Crest, 1956. Humor.

Peck, M. Scott. *The Road Less Traveled.* New York: Simon and Schuster, 1980. Surviving stress.

Peter, Laurence J., and Bill Dana. *The Laughter Prescription.* New York: Ballatine, 1982. Humor.

Post, Emily. *Etiquette: The Blue Book of Social Usage.* London and New York: Funk & Wagnalls Co., 1945.

Reinhold, Aman, ed. *Maledicta: The International Journal of Verbal Aggression.* Philadelphia: Running Press, 1987. Hostile humor, teasing, and insults.

Robinson, Vera. *Humor and the Health Professions.* N.J.: Charles B. Slack, 1977. Humor.

Sanborn, Jane. *A Bag of Tricks.* P.O. Box 167, Florissant, Colo. 80816: Search Publications, 1984. Noncompetitive games.

Siegel, Bernard S. *Love, Medicine and Miracles.* New York: Harper and Row, 1986. Surviving stress.

Styron, William. *Darkness Visible.* New York: Random House, 1990. Depression.

There Is a Rainbow Behind Every Dark Cloud. 19 Main Street, Tiburon, Calif. 94920: Center for Attitudinal Healing, 1978. Attitudinal Healing.

Toffler, Alvin. *Future Shock.* New York: Random House, 1970. Classic book on stress and rapid change.

Trueblood, Elton. *The Humor of Christ.* New York: Harper and Row, 1975. Humor.

Vaillant, George. *Adaptation to Life.* Boston: Little, Brown, 1977. Humor.

————. *The Natural History of Alcoholism: Causes, Patterns, and Paths to Recovery.* Cambridge: Harvard University Press, 1983. Alcoholism.

Weinstein, Matt, and Joel Goodman. *Everybody's Guide to Non-Competitive Play.* San Luis Obispo, Calif.: Impact Publishing, 1988. A book about play and fun, with directions for a variety of noncompetitive games.

Index

Framer, Axel, 236
France, 202, 236
Frankl, Viktor E., 219
Freud, Sigmund, 92, 179
Fries, James F., 249
Fry, William, 11–12

Gene (employee under stress),
   148–51
General adaptation syndrome,
   46–50
Goleman, Daniel, 166
Goodman, Joel, 139
Gordon, Jack, 156
GQ magazine, 244
Gramma (author's
   grandmother), 70, 77–78, 93,
   145, 177, 270
Greenberg, Lynn, 265, 266, 268
Grief, 28, 257–58, 268–70. *See
   also* Death
Grinspoon, Lester, 202, 208
Guilt, 79, 126, 140, 148, 168,
   214, 259,

Hageseth, Christian, 113, 143–
   44, 228–30
Hansel, Tim, 224
Haynes, Captain Alfred, 1–4, 6,
   69–70
Hendrix, Jimi, 241
Henton, John, 187
Heraclitus, 97
Hewlett-Packard, 170
Hill, Anita, 185–86
Hollywood movies, 3–4, 5, 37,
   51–52, 124
Hospice programs, 28–34, 94,
   131. *See also* Ed
Hostages, Mideast, 26, 103–4,
   108–9, 210
Howl for Joy, 143–46, 194, 216,
   222
Humaerobics, 52–65, 73, 113–
   22, 143–46, 194, 216, 222
Humor, contract, 190–93;
   definition of, 9, 26; etiquette

of, 5; Humor Inventory (HI),
   73–90; Humor library, 72–
   73, 281–85; positive versus
   negative, 194–95 ; as
   weapon, 15, 39, 75, 173, 174,
   187, 190
Humor seminar. *See* Seminars
Humor skills, learned, 5, 13–
   14, 16–40, 66, 68, 226, 232;
   definition of, 17; escaping
   from the center of the
   universe, 66–91; sense of joy,
   123–46 ; taking yourself
   lightly, 92–122

Illness, 18–25, 28, 263–64, 265.
   See also Cancer, Center for
   Attitudinal Healing, Death
Illusions, positive, 125–26
Imagination, 250. *See also*
   Minivacations, Visualization
Immune system, 49–50
International Research
   Associates, 170
Isen, Alice M., 10, 166
Ishii, Jun, 154
Italians, 202

Jacobsen, David, 103
Jampolsky, Jerry, 18, 20–23,
   25, 27, 34, 35, 39, 67, 68,
   224, 262
Japanese, and Japanese-
   Americans, 53, 151–54, 158,
   171
Jellinek, E.M., 200
Jenco, Father Lawrence
   Martin, 103–4
Jews, 202, 236
Johannsen, Mrs., 43–44
Jokes, 6, 14, 75, 180, 192;
   family, 184–85; racist, 178–
   80; sexist, 172–73
Joy, 13, 123–46; Joy List, 132–
   37, 143, 222, 253
Judd, Lewis L., 227
Juggling, 53, 138